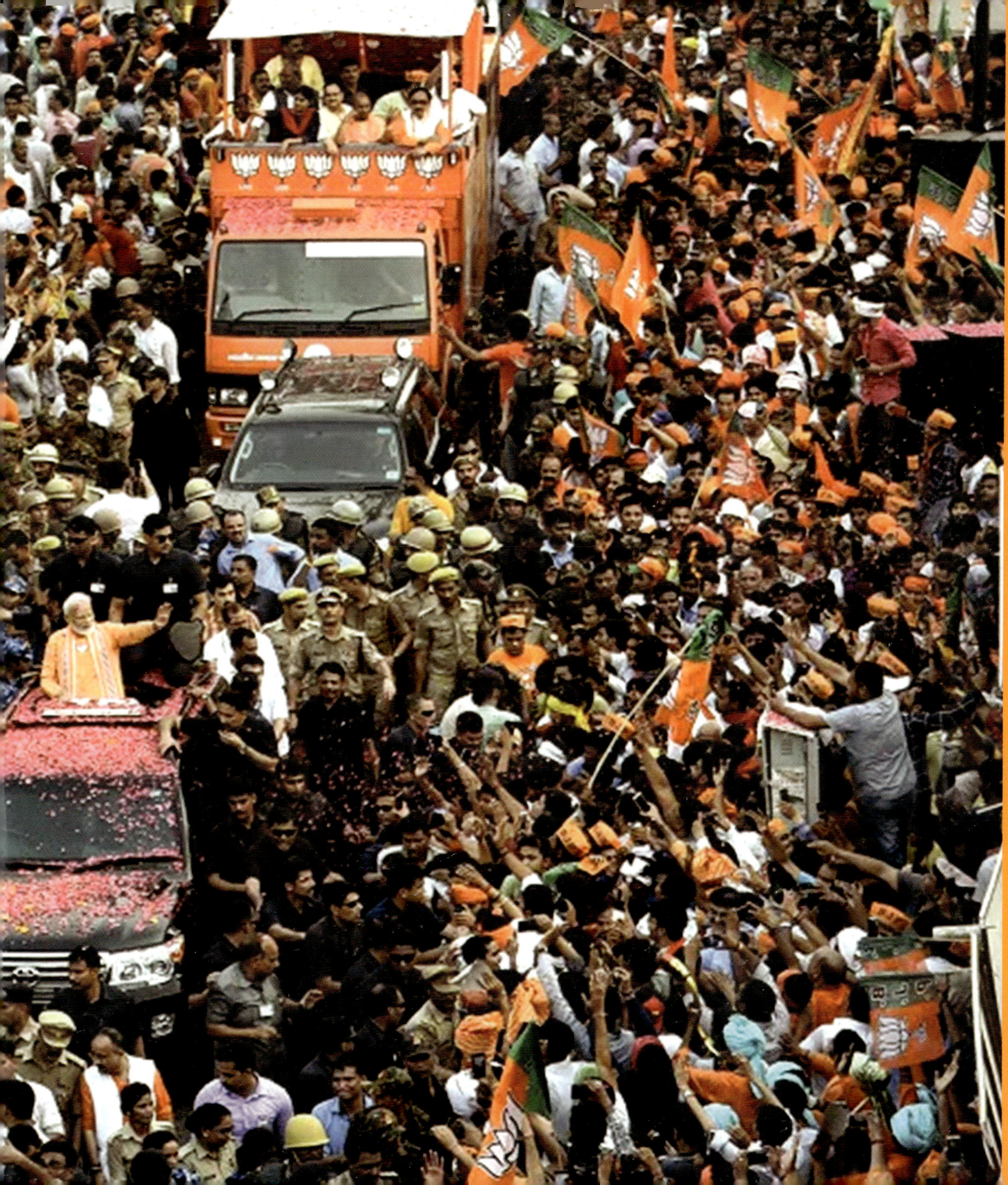

Renu Kaul Verma
Concept, Editing and Visualisation

Ratan Kaul
Advisor

Somesh Kumar Mishra
Design and Photo Research

The Modi Story

Perform
Reform
Transform

The Modi Story

Compiled and Edited by
Renu Kaul Verma

Vitasta

Published by
Vitasta Publishing Pvt Ltd
4348/4C, Ansari Road, Daryaganj
New Delhi - 110 002
info@vitastapublishing.com

ISBN 978-81-19670-27-7

MRP ₹3999

First Edition 2025

Printed at Nutech Print Services - India

CONTENTS

India has something to offer
for every kind of traveller -
from adventure seekers to
history buffs, from culture
enthusiasts to nature lovers.
—Narendra Modi

PREFACE

A lot has changed since *Being Modi* was published in 2014. After serving two terms, Narendra Modi has established himself as one of the most successful leaders of Independent India. His strong personality and diligence to work for the people has also ensured him the love of the public. Modi's increasing popularity and strides in taking the country forward has made it necessary that we expand this book to reflect his ongoing journey.

The newly added chapters highlight the struggles and achievements of the Modi administration. They take a close look at his relationship with the world leaders and how it has shaped his government's policies. From steering the country away from the hazards of Covid-19 pandemic to reinstating Lord Ram's temple in Ayodhya, Modi has shown himself mightily capable of cruising through several crises and fulfilling his promises to the people of the country. PM Modi's charismatic personality has become a catnip for the media. He has been extensively photographed and profiled by numerous publications as well. The revised brand new book *Perform.Reform.Transform: The Modi Story* includes snapshots of all the major events that have occurred in Modi's personal and professional life. It traces his trajectory from the swearing-in ceremony to swiftly rising among the ranks of leaders who are going to define this century.

Recent polls and electoral victories suggest that Modi's appeal transcends traditional voting patterns, with his personal brand often outshining his party's in many regions. As India's global stature rises, many people associate this ascent with Modi's leadership, further cementing his position as one of the greatest figures in Indian politics.

ACKNOWLEDGMENTS

We express our heartfelt gratitude to all our friends and well-wishers, with special recognition for Mrs Ratan Kaul, the esteemed founder of Public Diplomacy Forum and one of our valued advisors. Her persistent encouragement played a pivotal role in inspiring us to present the updated version of the book *Being Modi*, originally published in 2014.

A sincere thank you to Sudesh Verma, National Spokesperson of BJP, whose generosity in allowing us to utilise his notes for his latest book, *Transforming India: Gamechanger in Action,* assessing nine plus years of the Modi Government is truly appreciated. The fact that he granted permission to incorporate content from his earlier work *Narendra Modi The Gamechanger*, reflects his magnanimity.

Our gratitude also extends to Lawyer Nikita Parmar, whose passionate efforts in the original book were invaluable. I vividly remember our meeting with the then Chief Minister of Gujarat Shri Narendra Modi and how he swiftly directed his staff at the CM's house to open the archives for us. Nikita's Gujarati background further facilitated meaningful connections for the research.

Our thanks are also due to all those who supported the previous book. Shahnaz Husain not only wrote a Foreword for the book, she helped reach the book to the high and mighty.

Mrs Radha Bhatia, Mr Behram Mehta and journalist Abhilash Khandekar, a big thank you to all of you. Your steadfast support and contributions were instrumental in the success of the project, laying the foundation for us to complete a sequel.

Our sincere appreciation goes to all individuals, including Abhishek Rana and Saumya Chaudhary, who played a part in making this project a reality. Your support and collaboration have been instrumental in shaping the narrative of this book.

INTRODUCTION

Some are born great, some achieve greatness, and some have greatness thrust upon them, wrote William Shakespeare, the Bard of Avon, in his renowned play *Twelfth Night*.

When we turn our attention to analysing the Indian Prime Ministers, Narendra Modi has unequivocally demonstrated to the world that he has attained greatness through sheer determination, relentless hard work, and countless sleepless nights. His journey from serving tea to train passengers in Vadnagar in his childhood to assuming the role of the Prime Minister of India has been undeniably monumental.

Modi's trajectory has been marked by instances where he defied the odds and carved out history. A sage once prophesied that he would rise to prominence, a prediction that seemed distant and inconsequential amid his family's struggle to secure even two square meals a day.

Yet fate had a distinct plan for him. He ascended to the position of Chief Minister of Gujarat without holding a seat in either house of the State Legislature, an accomplishment made more remarkable by the fact that he had never contested an elected office before. He went on to serve as the Chief Minster four times before transitioning to the national stage, where he assumed office as the Prime Minister of India.

When he took the oath as Chief Minister for the fourth time in 2012, it was already a grand show at the Sardar Patel Stadium in Ahmedabad. The ceremony was viewed across 83 nations including the USA, the UK, Australia and Canada. Modi took a victory lap in the packed stadium. On 26 May 2014, as Narendra Modi assumed the role of prime minister, he stood atop a mountain of popularity never before scaled by an Indian leader. Representing a vast sea of humanity, he marked a historic moment by becoming the first Prime Minister ever who was not born in British India.

Indeed, he led the Bharatiya Janata Party to an unparalleled triumph, breaking a longstanding trend. Since 1984, no individual party had managed to secure an outright majority. The BJP's achievement was astounding, clinching 282 Lok Sabha seats in 2014, while the BJP-led National Democratic Alliance secured an even more impressive 336 Lok Sabha seats in 2019.

What propelled Modi to his remarkable victory was the profound hope that people vested in him and his vision for India: a blend of cultural resurgence and contemporary values. People recognised in him a beacon of assurance, a leader in whose hands the nation felt secure.

Modi earnestly strove to meet these towering expectations. He initiated a slew of pioneering pro-poor programmes previously unheard of in the country. His tenure was punctuated by transformative decisions that elevated India's global standing. Furthermore, he undertook measures to unleash the boundless creative potential within the nation's youth.

Five years later when he once again confronted the polls, the electorate rebuffed the opposition's relentless attacks and bestowed upon him an even more substantial mandate. This victory elevated him to the pinnacle of being India's most adored and revered leader.

In response to the Congress Party's unfounded allegations of *chowkidar chor hai* (The watchman is a thief), Modi ingeniously retorted by changing his display picture to *Mai bhi Chowkidar* (I am also a watchman), effectively turning their accusation into a statement of collective vigilance.

He secured an unprecedented victory for the BJP in the 2019 Lok Sabha elections. The party won 303 seats and the NDA won 353. The BJP also witnessed a substantial increase in its vote share. The opposition Congress won only 52 seats, which was not enough to give Rahul Gandhi the status of the leader of the Opposition. Narendra Modi took oath as Prime Minister of India for a second time on 30 May 2019.

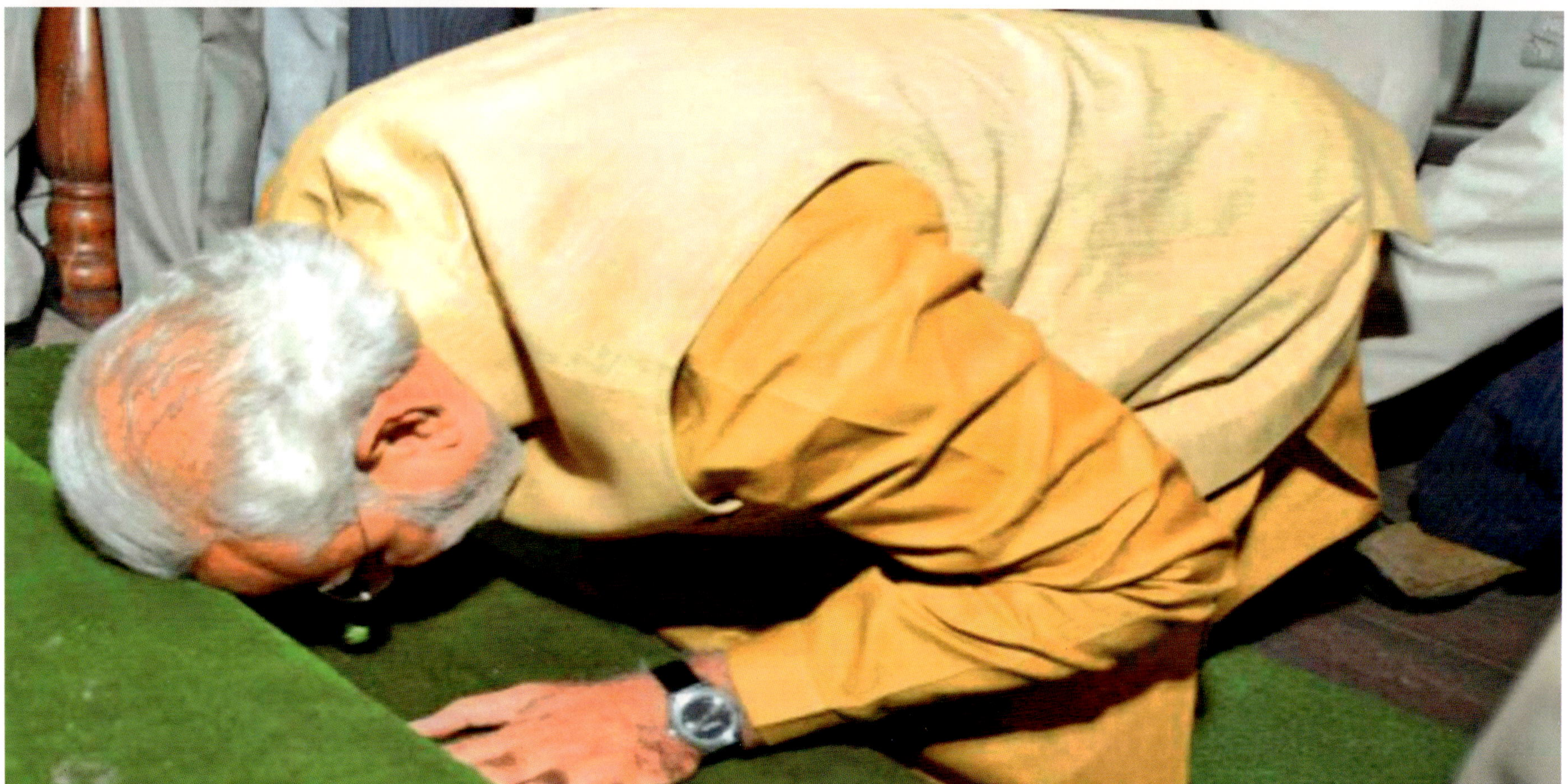

(Clockwise) PM Modi at the swearing-in ceremony in 2014 (left) and 2019 (right): He bowed in reverence as he entered the parliament for the first time (bottom)

THE EARLY YEARS...

VADNAGAR

NARENDRA DAMODARDAS Modi, beatifically addressed as NaMo by his fans, ND by friends, Kumar by his father, Narendrabhai by colleagues and Modi by others, was born on 17 September 1950 in a small village town of Vadnagar, about 100 km north of Ahmedabad. His mother Heeraben was a homemaker, and his father Damodardas ran a tea stall near the railway station.

They lived in a small house comprising two rooms, a half-wall partition in one to create space for a puja room and a kitchen. Damodardas had six children — five sons and a daughter. Modi was the third child after whom sister Vasanthi was born.

The family traces its roots to Rajasthan and belongs to a backward *Ghanchi* (Teli) caste (oil pressing caste).

Hiraba worked for a while at the houses of others filling water and cleaning utensils when the family fell on hard times.

The house where Modi grew up. The house was sold after 2001 and was renovated by its present owners

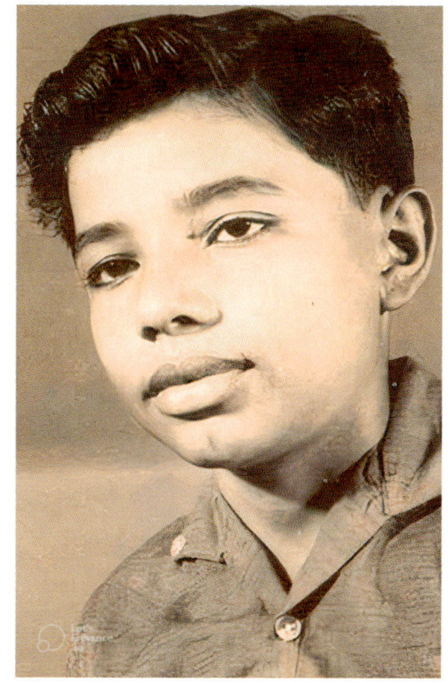

The place near the railway station where Modi's father ran a tea stall (left); PM Modi in childhood (right)

Instead of learning in school or playing with his friends and siblings, Modi had to spend most of his time at the tea stall. He began selling tea to railway passengers at the tender age of six. Modi would work at his father's stall and wait for the trains to come. He would rush out with an aluminium kettle and earthen glasses (*kulhad*). Even when he was in school trying to focus on the lessons being taught, he would keep an ear out for the whistle of the trains so that he could run from school and reach the station before the train arrived at the platform.

Modi began his schooling from Jethalal Joshi's Gamthi Shala, a school behind his house where he studied up to class IV. He completed the upper primary (Classes V-VII) from No. 1 Primary School commonly known as Durbar. For Classes VIII-XI, he joined the Bhagvatacharya Narayanacharya High School (BN High School).

For higher education, he moved to MN College at Visnagar, about 30 minutes from Vadnagar by train.

Modi joined the *Bal Shakhas* of the Rashtriya Swyamsewak Sangh (RSS) when he was a student of Class V. Interestingly, it was inquisitiveness and not ideology that drove him to the *shakhas*. His devotion to Swami Vivekananda, innate nationalism and unshakeable patriotism took birth during this time.

BN High School, Vadnagar, where Modi studied till classes VIII-XI

MN College, where Modi was enrolled for PUC and graduation (Top); View of the college entrance (Bottom)

Modi was also a part of the National Cadet Corps (NCC) during his schooling. The discipline that he is now known for was probably imbibed during that training.

After completing his matriculation, Modi shifted to a college in Visnagar for his higher education.

His favourite sport was swimming in the vast Sharmishtha Lake which, of course, led to a lot of parental censure because they feared the crocodile infested lake could prove fatal.

Counter clockwise: Narendra Modi among NCC Cadets; A group photo of Narendra Modi with his batchmates; Narendra Modi while enacting a role in a play called 'Hariyali Kranti' (Green Revolution) during his college days

14 Years Old Narendra Modi (left)
performing in the role of 19th century
Kathi Chieftain

THERE IS A STORY HERE....

In the middle of the lake is an old temple on which a saffron flag flutters with pride. It has been customary to get the flag changed during the *Bhadra Paksha* (an auspicious fortnight for Hindus) that falls in May-June during the peak of the monsoon season. The ritual also translates into a game where swimmers try to reach the top of the temple in order to change the flag. Coconuts are thrown on the sides of the swimmers to prevent crocodiles from coming closer. The crocodiles normally do not harm anyone, but during the peak of the monsoon anything could happen. The lake does not have any crocodile now. On one such auspicious day, when the monsoon was at its peak and the waters of the lake swelled dangerously high, a few young boys started swimming together to change the flag. The village elders were against this but no one paid heed to them. Three swimmers finally came back unsuccessful. But Narendra persevered, went to the top of the temple, changed the flag, swam back and simply walked away shrugging off looks of disbelief.

Sharmishta Lake and the temple in the middle, surrounded by circling crocodiles

EN ROUTE TO AHMEDABAD

MODI MOVED to Ahmedabad in 1971 to work as a cashier at a canteen because the life that he had envisioned for himself was not possible in Vadnagar.

This job probably laid the ground for his flight into political activism. As fate would have it, one day he saw some people near his canteen, protesting against fare hike in state transport buses. Modi went to them and met Ambalal Koshti for the first time. Koshti was then general secretary of Kankariya ward, Jan Sangh. As they grew closer, impressed by his passion and thoughts, Koshti made Modi general secretary, a position he himself held.

Modi also befriended a few RSS members who frequented the canteen. Through them he got in touch with Vakil Saheb (Laxman- Rao Inamdar), who had left an indelible mark on his mind when he was a child in Vadnagar. Vakil Saheb formally introduced Modi to the RSS and in 1972 asked him to shift to Hedgewar Bhawan, the RSS headquarters in

Ahmedabad, where *pracharaks* resided and morning *shakhas* were held. Modi would get up early in the morning, fetch milk, make tea for others, sweep the floor and prepare breakfast for all. But soon he graduated to handling the correspondence of RSS seniors and reserving train tickets for their travels.

Impressed by his debating skills and unquenchable thirst for knowledge, Vakil Saheb persuaded him to pursue higher studies even as Modi insisted he wanted to become a full- time worker of the RSS. In deference to his mentor, he joined BA correspondence course at Delhi University, something that proved to be of great use during the anti-Emergency agitation in the 1970s.

During the Bangladesh war, Modi participated in the agitation demanding action against the US for supporting Pakistan. A lesser known Modi, was soon arrested and sent to Tihar jail.

But given his nature, Modi made the best of this visit to Delhi too. He toured the Taj Mahal at Agra with his friends! At the same time, India and its people were agitating all through the country against corruption. Gujarat especially witnessed the anti-corruption Navnirman Movement that transformed into the biggest anti-Congress movement and overthrew the state government. Modi was assigned the job of supporting this movement where he stayed in touch with the Akhil Bharatiya Vidyarthi Parishad (ABVP) and other student bodies.

Hedgewar Bhawan, the RSS headquarters in Ahmadabad, where Modi stayed and worked in the beginning of his political career (left), The house where Modi stayed during the Emergency (right)

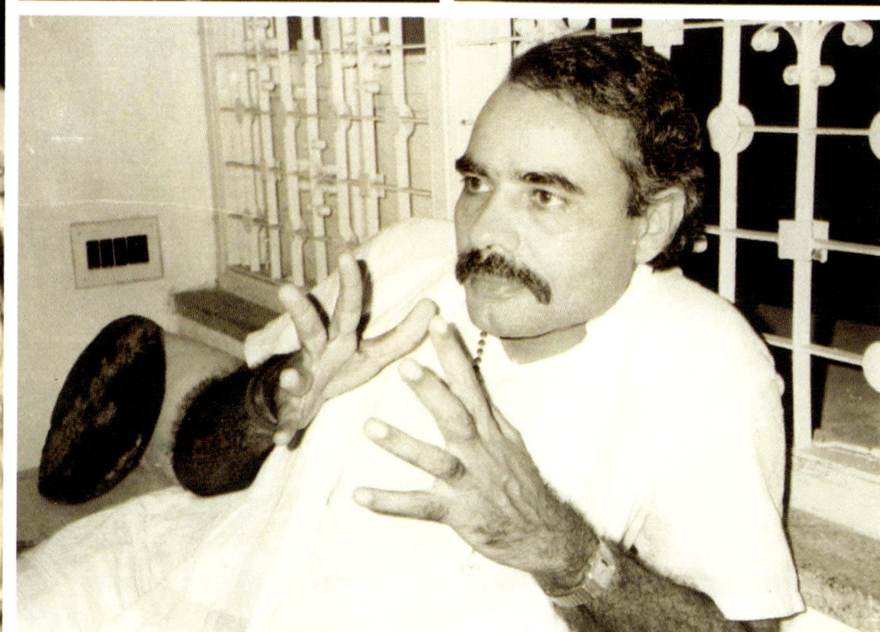

Gauging the unrest against the Congress, which had consumed the youth of the country, Jayaprakash Narayan, inspired by Gujarat, started a similar agitation in Bihar. A fearful Indira Gandhi promptly imposed the Emergency in 1975 and arrested many leaders overnight.

During the Navnirman Movement and later, Modi came in touch with Jayaprakash Narayan, Ravindra Varma, George Fernandes, Nanaji Deshmukh and other leading lights.

Vakil Sahib had asked Modi to stay underground and guide the movement much against the young man's wish to go to jail. This experience ensured that he learnt how to ensure the flow of information, organise secret meetings and influence international opinion. During this time, Modi edited a magazine called *Multavani* and wrote for *Sadhna*. To prevent detection, he continuously remained in disguise. He visited jails to interact with RSS workers and other political prisoners. During one such disguise he dressed like a Sardarji, and amused the children around, cutting Sardarji jokes to their hearts' content! While everyone was raring to enjoy the fruits of power after the Janata Party came to power in 1977, Modi underwent training at the RSS headquarters in Nagpur and became a full time *pracharak* the same year and a *vibhag pracharak* in 1978. He soon rose in the RSS hierarchy and at the same time completed his Masters in Political Science through correspondence from Gujarat University.

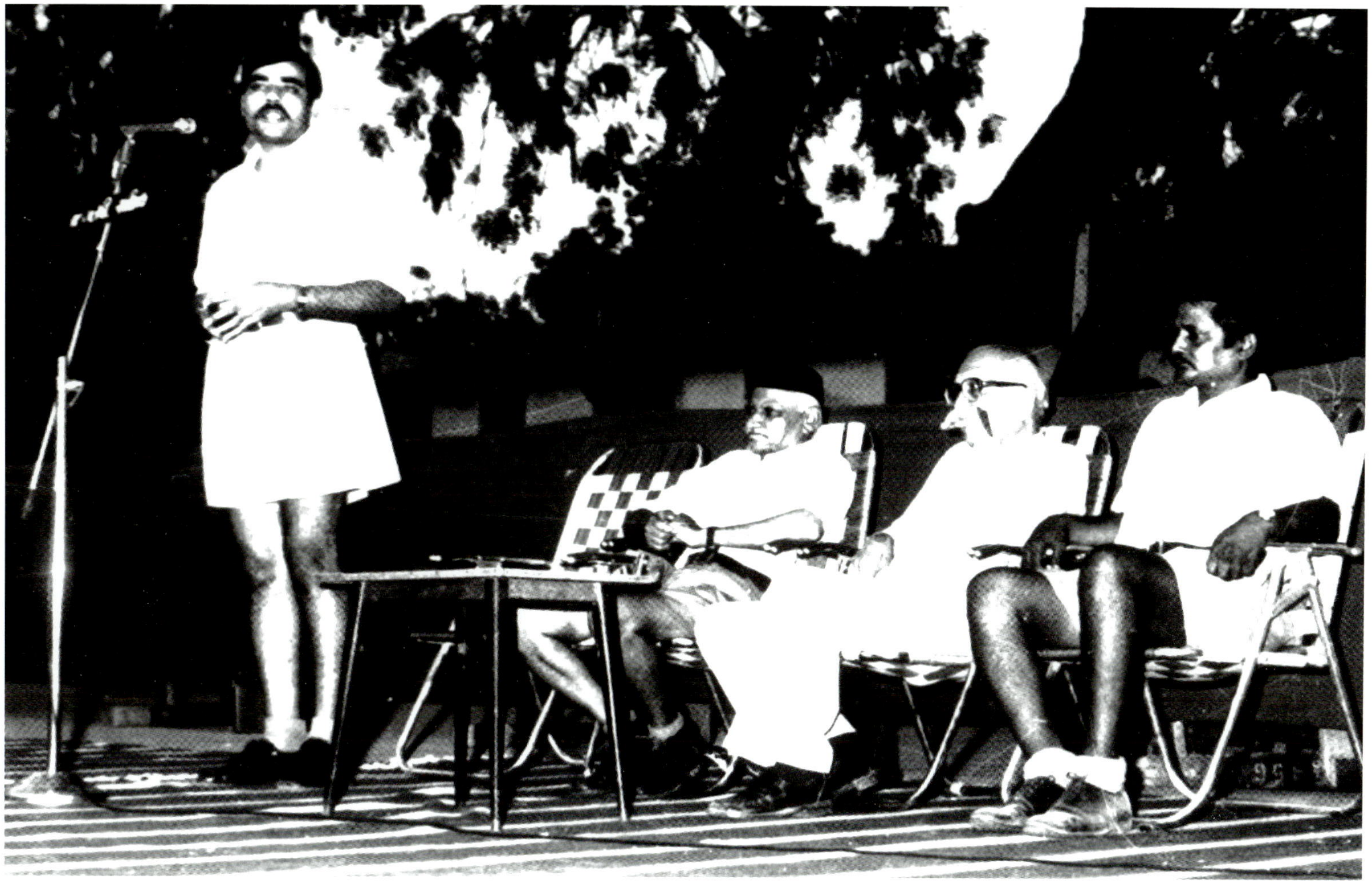

Modi at various stages in his life with the RSS. Rising from a helper to gaining the confidence of the organisation did not come easy

POLITICAL BAPTISM

WANTING TO systematically plan the BJP's rise as a strong political force, the new party president LK Advani, asked the RSS to suggest someone who was a good organiser. The choice automatically was the 37-year old Modi. He was made a secretary in 1987 and soon struck a chord with Advani, who was already the BJP's popular face.

This was his first test. Immensely impressed with two stalwarts of that time, Keshubhai Patel and Shankersinh Vaghela, Modi worked tirelessly with them and helped infuse the party with new energy.

When the state was caught in caste riots due to an anti-reservation stir that snow-balled into a major religious riot, there were large scale complaints of discrimination. After his induction into the BJP he came up with the concept of Nyaya Yatra to get justice for the riot victims. The other yatra he launched was the Lok Shakti Yatra towards early 1989 which became popular due to its fight against the city's liquor mafia in Ahmedabad.

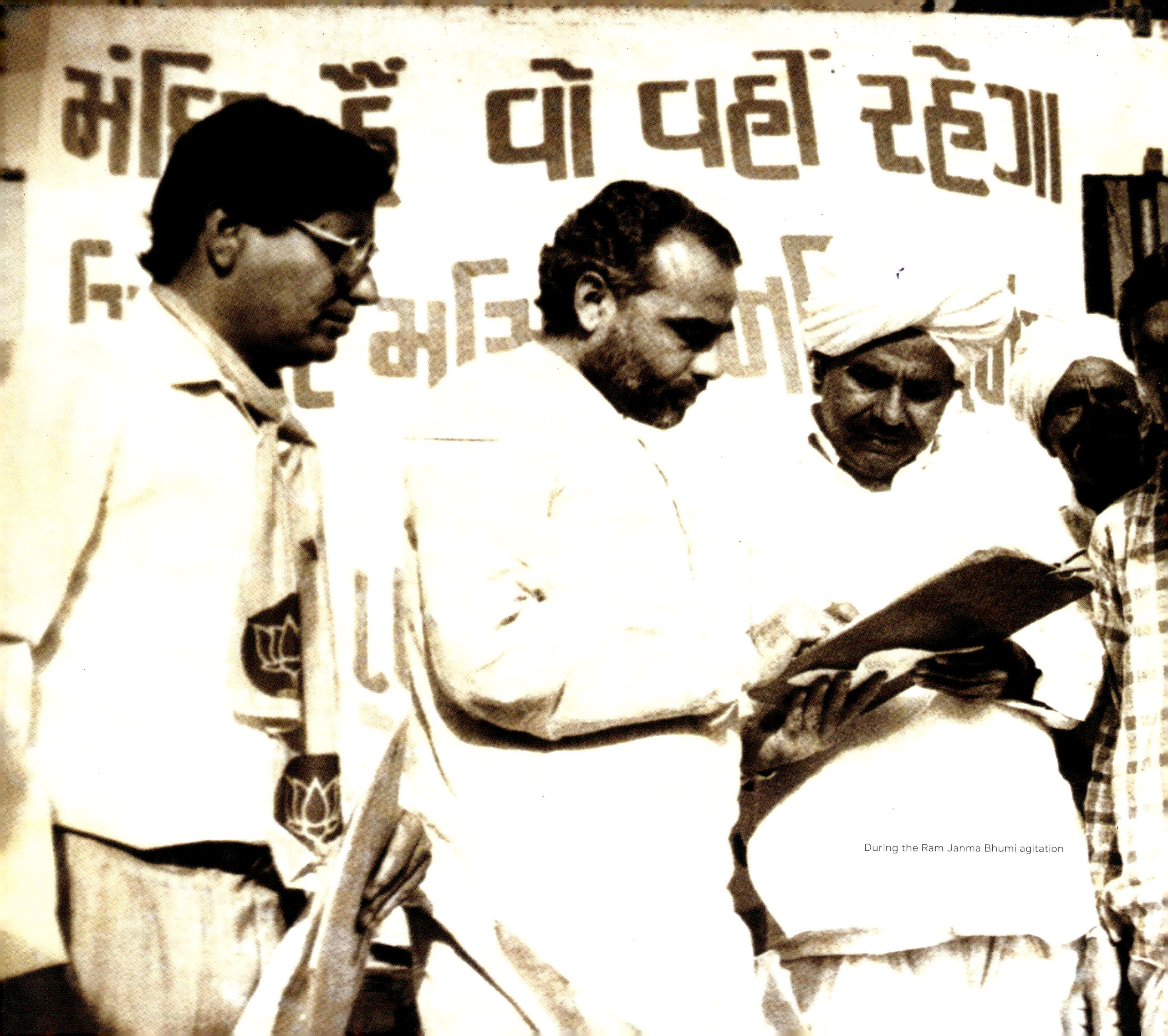

During the Ram Janma Bhumi agitation

He had already become the party's organising secretary for the state in 1988 and proved to be a better judge of the situation when the party won all 12 seats it contested in alliance with the Janata Dal, whereas the Janata Dal contested 14 but won from only 11. In the assembly elections that followed in January 1990, the BJP contested from 80 seats and the JD from 102. The BJP won 67 and the JD won 70.

Chimanbhai specifically met Modi to gauge what made the young man so sought after. Modi, as straightforward as he was, wanted Keshubhai to be made the Deputy Chief Minister, which Chimanbhai vehemently disagreed with. Patel remained clearly recognisable as the number two in the government. Modi was not comfortable with Chimanbhai's intransigence and privately decided to work towards carving a way for the BJP's rise to power on its own.

The year 1990 was eventful. When VP Singh drew the Mandal card in August, LK Advani backed by the RSS came up with the Ram Rath Yatra in September which was to begin from Somnath and end at Ayodhya. Modi was the charioteer in Gujarat and impressed everyone with his effective crowd management. The yatra elicited an unprecedented response where at some places people anointed Advani with *tilaks* of their blood. An overwhelmed Advani asked Modi to accompany him up to Mumbai. The yatra culminated in the arrest of LK Advani in Bihar and the consequent fall of the VP Singh Government.

Immensely impressed with the seniors, Modi worked tirelesslyand helped infuse the party with new energy

A Hero's welcome

In 1992, unfurling the *tiranga* at Lal Chowk in Srinagar, Jammu and Kashmir

Modi at Ekta Yatra

Recognition of Modi's organisational capacity reached its peak when Dr Murli Manohar Joshi became the national president of the BJP in 1991 and decided to launch the Ekta Yatra (Unity Yatra) on the issue of terrorism. The agenda was to hoist the Tricolor at the historic Lal Chowk in Srinagar on 26 January 1992. Modi, who had become a member of the party's national executive along with his responsibility in the state, was asked to organise the yatra nationally. It was a clear pat on the back that despite not being a national leader, Modi was asked to organise the yatra.

Modi gained in stature this time since he was not only a charioteer but also a speaker at most meetings. Highly impressed with his patriotic fervour, Joshi gave Modi pride of place alongside him when the national flag was hoisted at Lal Chowk, Srinagar. Modi returned to Gujarat a hero but faced in Vaghela his staunch detractor, since the latter was unhappy that Modi had supported Keshubhai for the number two position in the Chimanbhai government. That resulted in Vaghela keeping Modi out of his new team when he became the new president of the state unit. Undeterred, Modi channelised his energies into the conceptualisation and implementation of 'Samskar Dham, the school in memory of his mentor Vakil Saheb.

During this period, Modi convinced Advani to contest from the Gandhinagar Lok Sabha seat in 1991 and worked overtime to ensure his victory. When Advani became party president in 1992 and there was a change in the dispensation of the state unit in 1993, Modi was inducted as general secretary.

After this, Modi got involved in mobilising support to bring to fruition his mission to get a sound majority for the BJP. The dream was fulfilled in 1995 when the BJP won 121 of the 182 seats and Keshubhai became the Chief Minister of Gujarat. While Keshubhai ran the government, Modi continued to work at the organisational level to gain more victories for the party-this time round at the local elections signifying the BJP's complete sway over the electorate.

All this while Vaghela was still smarting at the fact that Keshubhai had not appointed many of Veghela's loyalists to important political posts in the government. In 1995 when Keshubhai was abroad on a foreign tour, there was a revolt in the party and 48 MLAs loyal to Vaghela flew off with him to Khajurao. The government could have come down but for the intervention of Atal Behari Vajpayee who struck a deal with Vaghela. Keshubhai was forced to step down and a compromise candidate Suresh Mehta was made the Chief Minister. Modi, caught in the vortex of political factionalism was ironically blamed by both Keshubhai and Vaghela for the crisis. To keep the party together, he was banished to Delhi as a national secretary. Keshubhai was made the national vice-president but continued to stay in Ahmedabad.

DELHI YEARS

MODI SPENT the next six years in Delhi. During that time he preferred not to go to Gujarat. At times, when the love for his home could not keep him away, he avoided visiting the RSS and BJP headquarters fearing that he might be misunderstood. He would only visit Samskar Dham for a few days to ensure its smooth functioning and after satisfactory interaction with students, catch the next train back to Delhi.

The years in Delhi witnessed his rise to the post of general secretary organisation. In 1998, he worked as in-charge of most states of North India like Punjab, Haryana, Himachal Pradesh, Jammu and Kashmir and the Union Territory of Chandigarh. That year, Advani asked him to campaign for the party in Gujarat and yet again Modi proved his mettle when the BJP won and Keshubhai became the Chief Minister.

When in Delhi, Modi stayed at the residence of a BJP MP Dilip Sanghani. He also stayed in Chandigarh and encouraged the cadre to perform better.

His tenure saw the installation of Bansi Lal as Chief Minister of Haryana with the BJP's support and later Om Prakash Chautala, with whom he shared a good rapport.

In Himachal Pradesh, the creation of a youth brigade by him ensured the formation of a coalition government under Prem Kumar Dhumal. In Chandigarh, the BJP won the 1996 municipal elections for the first time with a thumping majority. They also won the Lok Sabha elections from Chandigarh in 1996. By the end of the 1999 Lok Sabha elections, everyone had started giving credit to Modi for delivering results wherever he went.

The BJP-led NDA Government had come to power at the Centre in 1998 but unfortunately the nation had to fight the Kargil war in 1999. In 2001, Pakistani President General Musharraf visited India to attend the Agra summit with Atal Behari Vajpayee but sabotaged the process due to his aggressiveness. When the NDA government drew flak for the failure of the Agra summit, Modi emerged as a strong defender of the decision on behalf of the party. It was then that his ire against General Musharraf went public and Modi charged the Pakistani President with promoting terrorism in India. It is well-known that Modi never used his position to get any favour from the government while the NDA was in power from 1998-2004. Whenever he would meet anyone, it would be for the cause of the party. During this time he shifted to the residence of Arun Jaitley which was being used by the party to house its pracharaks and guests where a special one room was allotted to him. This move proved lucky since it was from there that he was catapulted straight to the chair of the Chief Minister of Gujarat.

Samskar Dham School, Ahmedabad

CHIEF MINISTER

TACKLING OBSTACLES

NARENDRA DAMODARDAS MODI Modi became the first ever RSS *pracharak* to become a Chief Minister. Another *pracharak*, Sundar Singh Bhandari, was the governor who had sworn in Modi as the Chief Minister on 7 October 2001—a rare moment in the history of the RSS. With more than 50,000 party workers attending the swearing-in ceremony, it was a mega show. Rajnath Singh, the then Chief Minister of Uttar Pradesh, then Union Ministers LK Advani, Ram Vilas Paswan, Arun Jaitley, Dr Murli Manohar Joshi, George Fernandes and the then BJP National President Jana Krishnamurthy were present. Not one to ever ignore the cadre, Modi went to meet them in an open jeep. However, he was soon faced with his biggest challenge in the form of the horrific 2001 earthquake in Gujarat – a calamity so large in scale that state resources proved inadequate to tackle such a crisis. But with his usual pragmatism, Modi proved his mettle by organising relief and rehabilitation on an unmatched scale. Within six months of becoming the Chief Minister he got elected as a member of the legislative assembly. He contested for the first time in life and won from the Rajkot seat in February 2002.

That victory remained short-lived. Soon the state witnessed unprecedented violence, first in Godhra where 59 *Ramsewaks* were charred to death in a train, and later when the state was engulfed in the post-Godhra riots. A troubled Modi did everything he could to control the situation but the violence was so intense that it took some time for the state machinery to normalise the situation. While his critics were shouting at the top of their voices blaming him for failing to prevent the tragedy, the Chief Minister insisted he had done everything that was under administrative command. Modi's swearing-in as Chief Minister took place again in 2002, 2007 and 2012 as he continued to win elections one after the other despite every prediction of severe defeat. He launched the Gujarat Gaurva Yatra and spoke of the pride of the five crore people of Gujarat. People trusted what he said and rejected the critics. He won the 2012 elections with a landslide majority. Despite the friendly atmosphere of the Agra Summit to reaffirm his unwavering stance against terrorism, he persistently referred to General Parvez Musharraf as "Mia Musharraf" throughout the campaign. In every successive election, Modi proved his detractors wrong and changed the agenda from narrow considerations of caste, creed and religion to national development. While his critics spoke of other issues, he spoke of security and peace. On 1 June 2007, Modi completed 2063 days in office and became the longest serving Chief Minister of Gujarat. Modi is successful simply because good governance and development have been his main focus. Whatever Modi promised, he delivered. The population of the state had now swelled to six crore and when Modi spoke of the pride of six crore Gujaratis, the majority of them showed their trust in him and voted him back for the 3rd consecutive time in 2012.

Modi dissolved the Gujarat assembly in July 2002 to silence his critics and seek a fresh mandate. Modi won a landslide. He is seen completing the victory leap. With supporters after his swearing in for the second time in December 2002.

AN ABLE ADMINISTRATOR

WHETHER ONE is made Chief Minister or a Prime Minister, one's effectiveness and efficiency to govern is directly proportional to one's abilities to handle the country's huge bureaucracy. The inefficiency of Gujarat's bureaucracy was highlighted by the media during the earthquake relief and rehabilitation work. It was a challenge for Modi to make the same officials work effectively. Modi had a few initial tough months as Chief Minister but his training in the RSS and logical thinking helped him resolve many of these issues. He became an attentive student, learnt the ropes quickly and soon turned the tables on the very same bureaucrats who had earlier tried to laugh at his ignorance. This is how a bureaucrat described the transformation: "He was a sponge. He sat, listened, absorbed for a year. It is not as if he was assimilated or diluted by us. It is as if he domesticated and colonised us. He remained a pracharak but the secretariat became a magnified pracharak's world. We became a cadre of clerks, a shakha of bureaucrats." In whatever way the state bureaucracy works is a reflection of the leader. The underlying fact is that bureaucracy functions only when the babus know that the person sitting at the apex is a no-nonsense man. Modi infused tremendous confidence in the bureaucracy by giving officials their due importance, allowing them a fixed tenure, stopping political interference and doing away with 'middlemen' in transfers and postings. He encouraged out of the box thinking for pressing issues by organising Chintan Shibirs on a regular basis since 2003. Top bureaucrats and all ministers were referred to as members of 'Team Gujarat' and they had to put their minds together to innovate. Modi allowed them to go wrong provided they took decisions for the welfare of people. A rare happening for any other state, yet a common sight in Gujarat is to see more than 3000 officials, ministers and elected representatives led by the Chief Minister, walk into various villages and towns to get children enrolled in government primary schools. The concept of Chintan Shibir "Not I but We" is visible to one and all. He brought in the Karmayogi scheme to train government officials. The intention was to convert all five lakh state government employees into self-motivated performers by making their lives more meaningful.

He disproved the assumption that the typical official lacks motivation to work. They were encouraged to work extra hours. The opposition calculated they would vote against Modi. But, more than 75 per cent government employees voted for Modi in 2012 and proved everyone wrong.

He introduced e-Governance at every level of state administration. People in Gujarat say that a farmer can get a copy or his land record delivered to him in his village by paying a nominal fee, simply because e-Gram has computerised all land records. Other schemes such as e-Dhara also help in providing various services to people at their doorstep.

The much talked-about scheme which other states could and should emulate is the SWAGAT complaint redressal mechanism, handled by the Chief Minister's office. People whose issues have been pending for a long time can directly approach the CMO and register a complaint. And on the same day, the officials are instructed to be ready with their answers. The CM will sit with the complainant and discusses the case with officials through video conferencing. This happens on the third Thursday of every month.

The Team Gujarat at one of the Chintan Shibris organised at the Rann of Kutch

THE DEVELOPMENT MAN

IMAGINE DEVISING a proactive approach to state development despite facing a near-empty treasury. Gujarat was a revenue deficit state when Modi became its Chief Minister. Funds were not easily available since the state was defamed first for alleged tardy relief and rehabilitation during the earthquake and later, when the state witnessed large-scale riots in 2002.

Modi then came up with a novel concept of the Vibrant Gujarat Summit—inviting investors to understand the efforts of the new administration and invest in the state's development. He visited various countries and sent his ministers to do the same in order to clear misgivings about the state. Industrialists and top officials of Gujarat always accompanied him to showcase the state as a new investment destination.

Soon enough, the biennial summit became an important instrument for change and got fully institutionalised. It has now become a platform for knowledgeable information interchange for international business players.

Ratan Tata once famously said, 'If you are not in Gujarat (for investment) you are stupid.'

Getting these investors was extremely difficult as they were not keen to come to Gujarat. The situation changed after the state began to get noticed for good governance and soon created infrastructural facilities that did not exist earlier. Industrialists basically look for regular power and water supply and a responsive bureaucracy, which were issues that Gujarat tackled systematically one after the other. The loss-making GSEB was transformed into a profit-making enterprise. Gujarat became a power surplus state due to massive investment in the power sector. By an intricate system of canal networks, the water of the river Narmada was taken to remote corners of the state including various river basins, especially the river Sabarmati that had dried up and was no better than a backyard drainage canal. Herculean efforts to increase the level of the water table were carried out. Dams were built that prevented water from flowing into the rivers and the aquifers got charged up.

A better water table and an exemplary irrigation system created less dependence on power. Regular supply of power through a separate feeder ensured better power and water management. Farmers in Gujarat have been paying for the power they consume through a separate meter – a huge achievement which unfortunately none of the other state governments have yet been able to implement.

Gujarat is fast becoming a state that will show our country the way to developing an alternative source of energy. Solar energy is the future and the state has already become the leader by getting the first canal top solar power project. The state has also encouraged solar energy production by private players. One of them is cine actor Ajay Devgn, who has invested in a solar project. Very soon every house in Gandhinagar will be producing solar energy for domestic consumption and also selling the extra energy to the government grid. Gandhinagar is now slated to be the country's first city to become fully powered by solar energy.

Agriculture has been the priority of Gujarat. It is no wonder then that the state is growing at a rate of 9.6 per cent for the last 10 years. The state has a soil health card to tell farmers what and when it is conducive to grow a particular crop.

TATA nano

Modi overseeing developments across different sectors in Gujrat

Modi knows that agriculture must flourish to sustain industrial production. Empowerment of farmers has fuelled demand for consumer goods. In 2013, the Chief Minister organised the international agriculture summit. Innovative farmers from all over India attended the summit and were exposed to new technology and innovations in agriculture. Gujarat has encouraged skill development in a major way. There are skill training centres at the village levels and the majority of participants are women. Training is imparted as per the needs of the new industries that are coming up. Gujarat is the only state that issues prepaid skill vouchers for employers who want trained manpower. It allocated Rs 800 crore in 2013-14 for skill development whereas the central government allocated only Rs 1000 crore for the entire country. This is a testament to the state's commitment to skill development and, in turn, rural and women's progress.

It would be a dichotomy that a state with so many positives scores poorly on social indicators. The adverse female sex-ratio that alarmed the state and policy makers has now started to get equalised. Child sex ratio has improved and infant mortality has reduced. The ongoing Beti Bachao Abhiyan launched by the Chief Minister has created statewide awareness. Modi keeps reminding people to take care of their daughters and not treat them as a burden. His missionary zeal is seen when he takes part in the Kanya Kelavani campaign every year. Within the schemes for women in every field, there are appointments for women forest assistants to take care of the Gir forests and conductors to take care of bus transport.

Today, Gujarat also has good indicators in school enrolment. There was a fracas when the recent CAG report spoke of malnutrition in the state as being very high. The same CAG report then showed that the trend showed a steep decline that no other Indian state had witnessed. While Mission Balam Sukham has been tackling malnutrition, Mission Mangalam is ensuring that rural women learn new skills and get integrated into the value chain.

PRIME MINISTER

THE CEO MODI

SPLENDID VISION, unmatched organisational skills, being a great team leader, immaculate planning, entrepreneurial style of working, courage to take tough calls, administrative panache, an ability to lead from the front, understanding the pulse and being a people's person. No wonder, fortified with the above-mentioned virtues and more, the much deserving Narendra Modi has taken over as the CEO of India-the world's largest democracy.

Like any global CEO, Modi also displays unconventional thinking, deep-rooted conviction, an ability to redefine the playing field, being a staunch believer of his vision and completely fearless. From his dressing style, love for technology to flamboyant oratory skills, he has always differentiated himself from his peers and made a memorable impression on everyone who perceives him. Like a true leader, he has managed all fronts effectively, effortlessly and with a benign smile. Soft yet firm, he has always been in sync with the mood of the nation.

Modi's solid presence and his ability to sway the masses with his words have helped him secure the role of Prime Minister three times in a row.

After his triumph in 2019, Modi ran for his third term in the 2024 General Elections, held from 19 April to June. BJP won 240 seats out of a total 542, and retained its position as India's leading party. Modi became the Prime Minister of India for the third time consecutively. His showmanship and power as a charismatic speaker was on full display in his speeches during his rallies. He expertly demolished the opposition's talking points and presented his vision of India's future with a clarity that won the public's votes.

Swearing-in: SAARC leaders in attendance

Narendra Modi's swearing-in ceremony as the 14th Prime Minister on 26 May 2014 was a special occasion, as it was for the first time that swearing-in ceremony for an Indian PM was attended by the heads of SAARC (South Asian Association for Regional Cooperation) countries. The ceremony was held at the forecourts of the Rashtrapati Bhavan, Delhi. It was also the first time that the swearing-in was live-streamed on YouTube.

SAARC leaders in attendance for Modi's swearing-in ceremony as PM of India

Prime Minister Modi and Pakistani PM Nawaz Sharif in New Delhi in May 2014

Red Fort Address

In his maiden address from the Red Fort, as the country celebrated its 68th Independence Day, Prime Minister Narendra Modi articulated a vision of progress, inclusivity, and empowerment, setting the stage for a transformative era in India's history.

Central to the address was the importance of leveraging technology to streamline both public and private processes. The Pradhanmantri Jan-Dhan Yojana for instance, aimed at ensuring financial inclusion for every stratum of society across the country. Under this scheme, Modi promised that every poor family would be connected to a bank account, that'd keep their money safe and

A panoramic view from the Minarets of Red Fort on the occasion of 68th Independence Day

provide them with a debit card and a safety net of Rs 1 lakh through an accompanying insurance scheme.

Addressing the pressing need for cleanliness and sanitation, Modi launched the *Swachh Bharat Abhiyan* (Clean India Campaign), emphasising the government's commitment to promoting hygiene practices nationwide.

To bridge the digital divide and foster connectivity, Modi unveiled his vision of a Digital India envisaging internet access for everyone to facilitate learning, work and commerce, transcending geographical barriers.

Underscoring the importance of self-reliance, Modi championed the Make in India initiative, and highlighted the need to harness the nation's abundant skill, talent, discipline, and determination that the people possessed to bolster domestic production and global competitiveness.

The Prime Minister also raised concerns about women's safety, pledging robust measures to safeguard their rights and dignity.

PM Modi ended his speech by invoking Vivekananda's famous words that India's ultimate duty is to work toward the welfare of the world and called upon every citizen to help realise this destiny.

In his first Independence speech as the PM of India in 2014, Narendra Modi articulated his idea of India to the people of the country.

सत्यमेव जयते	सत्य की ही जीत होती है।	Truth Alone Triumphs
अहिंसा परमो धर्मः	अहिंसा ही सबसे बड़ा धर्म है|	Non-violence is the topmost Dharma
पौधों में परमात्मा दीखना	पौधों में परमात्मा देखना|	God seen even in Plants
आ नो भद्राः क्रतयो यन्तु विश्वतः	हमारी तरफ़ सब ओर से शुभ विचार आएँ।	Let good thoughts come from everywhere - from all the world
सर्व पंथ समभाव	सभी धर्मों को एक समान मानना ।	All Spiritual Paths are treated Equally
वसुधैव कुटुम्बकम्	पूरा विश्व एक परिवार है।	The whole World is one single Family
सर्वे भवन्तु सुखिनः सर्वे सन्तु निरामयाः	सब लोग सुखी हों ,सभी निरोग हों ।	May all be prosperous and happy May all be free from illness

Modi's vision: My idea of India (articulated in his first Independence day speech, other speeches and Mann ki Baat)

WELFARE SCHEMES

LIKE A true leader, the Modi administration has walked the talk in the past decade. The government has implemented numerous welfare measures benefitting the poor and the downtrodden, including cash subsidies via *Jan Dhan Yojna*, *Ayushman Bharat*, *Ujjwala Yojna*, housing for the poor, *Swachh Bharat* and toilet construction

Health Infrastructure

Ayushman Bharat Digital Mission aims to create a digital health infrastructure for every citizen. This includes a unique 14-digit *Ayushman Bharat* Health Account (ABHA) number accessible through Aadhar Card registration. Over 45 crore (ABHA) numbers have already been issued, facilitating quicker diagnosis and treatment through digital health records.

The poor often fall into a debt trap when grappling with a health crisis. The Modi government understood this and ensured cashless health insurance to 10 crore families. It covers treatment costs up to five lakh rupees, with the central government funding 60 per cent and states funding 40 per cent (90 per cent in the North-East and 100 per cent in Union Territories).

The government also established AIIMS like institutions across states. It opened new medical colleges, and seeks to have a super-specialty hospital in each Lok Sabha constituency.

Ujjwala Gas

The *Ujwala Yojna*, launched in 2016, aimed to provide clean cooking gas to impoverished women, improving health and reducing firewood use. It has benefitted 9.59 crore women, offering free LPG connections and equipment as well as subsidy for 12 cylinders.

और प्राकृतिक गैस मंत्रालय
भारत सरकार
उज्ज्वला योजना
के अन्तर्गत
8 करोड़वां

Before its launch, Modi initiated the 'Give it Up' campaign in 2015, urging the rich to surrender their LPG subsidies. Nearly one crore people responded, reducing the number of subsidised connection from 15.34 crore to support the scheme.

In 2020, general LPG subsidies were removed but *Ujjwala* beneficiaries continued to receive Rs 200 per cylinder subsidy.

Housing for All

The ambitious housing scheme strives to provide homes for all by 2024, targeting the homeless, Economically Weaker Section (EWS), and Low Income Group (LIG).

The programme includes *Pradhan Mantri Awas Yojna – Urban* (PMAY-U) and *Pradhan Mantri Awas Yojna – Gramin* (PMAY-G), administered by different Ministries. Funding is shared between the Centre and states (60-40 ratio) 90:10 for the North East and full funding for the Union Territories.

Beneficiaries are identified based on the 2011 census data. The scheme integrates various amenities like water, electricity, toilets, LPG connections, and bank accounts. Employment provisions are also in place to support job opportunities.

Remarkable progress has been made, with 2.13 crore rural houses built out of the 2.95 crore targeted. In urban areas, 55 per cent of the target has been achieved with a goal to complete by the end of 2024. The government allocated Rs 79.590 crore in the 2023-24 budget to accelerate the mission, totaling over Rs 2 lakh crore.

The Housing for All scheme empowers the poor and middle class, fulfilling a basic need and reducing homelessness. It has been seen as a game changer in the fight against poverty, creating a sense of pride and home for many.

Pradhan Mantri Sauchalay Abhiyan Yojana

Another remarkable milestone of the Modi decade has been the near abolition of open defecation. By constructing millions of toilets and advocating behavioural change, the initiative has ensured access to toilets for every household, particularly in rural areas, promoting hygiene, health, and dignity. It has empowered communities, especially women and girls, by providing safe and private sanitation facilities. Girls have started going to school in large numbers after the initiative was taken up in a big way.

JAGRITI

Narendra Modi launches Clean India Campaign by sweeping street

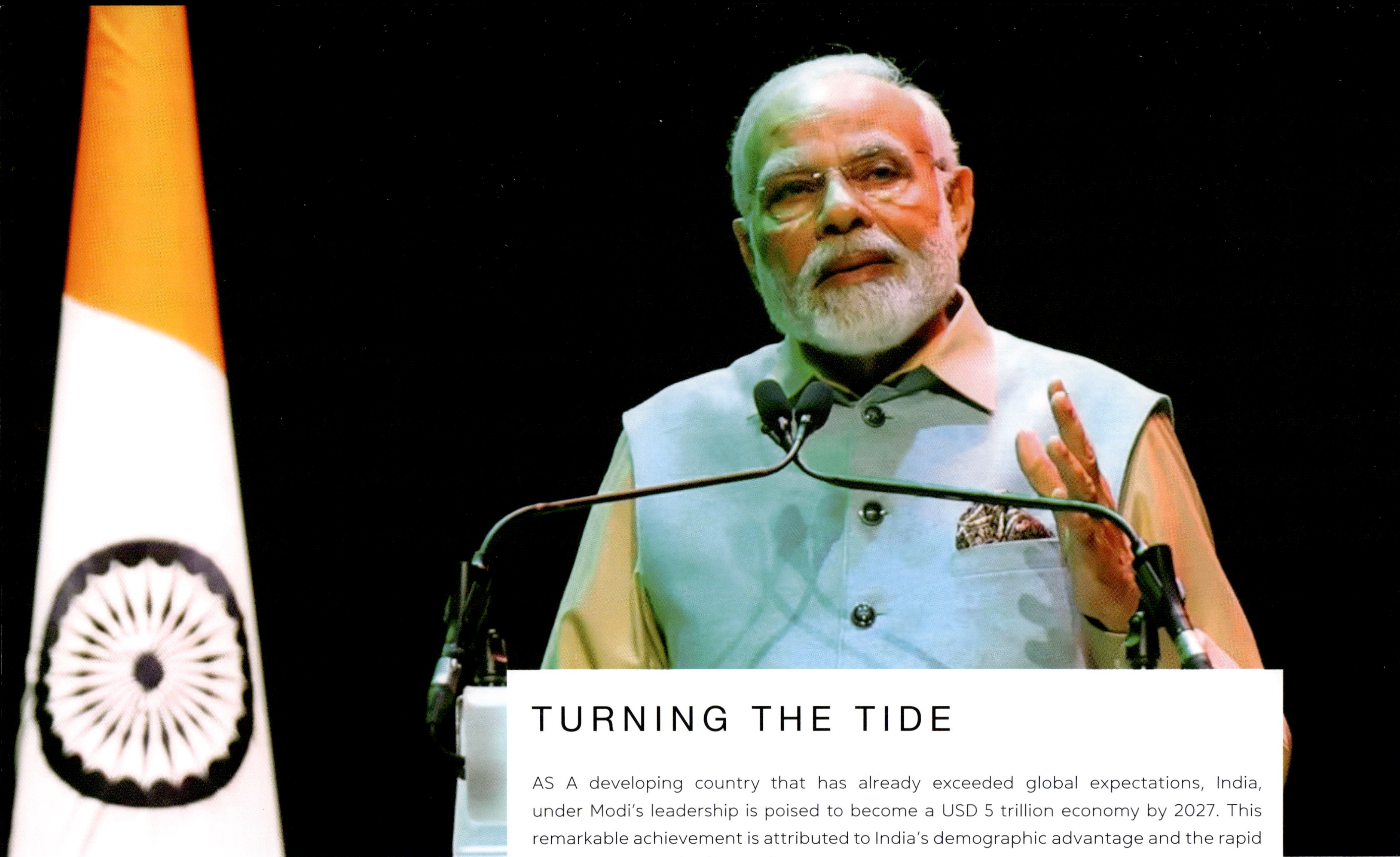

TURNING THE TIDE

AS A developing country that has already exceeded global expectations, India, under Modi's leadership is poised to become a USD 5 trillion economy by 2027. This remarkable achievement is attributed to India's demographic advantage and the rapid development in the financial sector.

With a vision to transform India into a developed nation by 2047, Prime Minister Modi has laid down ambitious plans to establish sustainable infrastructure capable of rivaling that of developed countries.

Central among these is the *Gati Shakti* programme which aims at consolidating major mobility infrastructure projects across central and state governments. These include *Bharatmala* (roads & highways), *Sagarmala* (a network of ports), inland waterways development, and the expansion of regional airports through the *Ude Desh ka Aam Nagrik* (UDAN) scheme, facilitating air travel accessibility for the common man.

GATI SHAKTI MASTER PLAN

Roadways capacity to be increased

Railways transport cargo capacity to be increased to **1,600 tonnes** by FY25

Renewable capacity to be increased to **225 GW** by FY25

Around 200 new airports, heliports and water aerodromes envisioned

Transmission network to be increased to **4,54,200 circuit km**

4G connectivity for villages by FY22. **Around 20** new mega food parks

Significant strides have already been made in the construction of national highways connecting all passenger, trade and freight points. In 2023-24 alone, an impressive 13,800 km of highways were conceptualised with an expenditure of Rs 2.81 lakh crore, an increase of 33 per cent from the previous year.

To transform India into a unified market, the NDA government has launched several ground breaking initiatives.

e-NAM is an online trading platform for agricultural commodities at the state and national level that promotes uniformity and streamlines procedures across integrated markets, removes information asymmetry between buyers and sellers and facilitates real-time price discovery.

GST implementation marks a significant milestone, introducing a single tax framework for the supply of goods and services, right from the manufacturer to the consumer. By allowing input credits at each stage of value addition, GST fundamentally taxes only the value added at each stage. GST ensures that indirect tax rates and structures are consistent across the country, thereby increasing certainty and ease of doing business.

e-NAM

National Agriculture Market

Making Lives Easier For Annadata

Benefits To Farmers:

- No middleman between farmers and buyers
- No dependency on anyone for the sale of crops
- Better prices for their produce
- Real-time progress of bids in mandis
- Time-saving, as farmers don't have to go to market for selling produce

Digital India, a campaign to provide internet services to all regions of India, was launched by Prime Minister Modi on 1 July 2015. The aim of the campaign was to develop a robust digital infrastructure, deliver government services digitally, and promote universal digital literacy.

Digital India synergises with various other schemes such as BharatNet, Make in India, Startup India, Standup India, *Bharatmala Sagarmala* and *Amrit Bharat Station Scheme*. The Government of India organisation Bharat Broadband Network Limited (BBNL) which operates over the BharatNet project is the prime custodian of the Digital India (DI) project.

DI has revolutionised communication and knowledge-sharing among citizens, enabling transactions through platforms like UPI, and democratising access to a wealth of information for those eager to learn.

PhonePe
ACCEPTED HERE

PM Modi stresses the important role that technology plays in shaping the future. From space to deep sea missions, *Vande Bharat* trains, electric buses, metro trains, villages getting internet, and semiconductor manufacturing, India is steadily working towards fulfilling all its aims for a transformed technologically forward country.

6th Vande Bharat

MOMENTOUS MILESTONES

CULTURAL REAWAKENING

NARENDRA MODI is arguably the first Prime Minister since India's Independence who has unapologetically pushed to bring the country's cultural heritage into national and international focus, turning this effort into a mission.

The construction of Ram Temple in Ayodhya stands as a defining moment in Modi's tenure, highlighting his leadership, resolve, and ability to navigate the complex socio-political landscape to achieve this historic milestones. The temple fulfills a long-standing aspiration of millions of Hindus and marks the resolution of a 500-year old dispute over the site. The Modi Government navigated legal complexities and societal sensitivities to pave the way for the temple's construction. By championing the cause of the temple, Modi not only honoured the sentiments of millions but also solidified his image as a leader who delivers on promises, especially those deeply rooted in the country's cultural and religious ethos.

Consecration ceremony of Ram Lalla in Ayodhya

PM Modi creating history with the inauguration of Ram Mandir at Aydhdhya

Revitalising Kashi Vishwanath Corridor, Mahakal, Char Dham Highway, Somnath Temple and now GyanVyapi reflects Modi's commitment to reassertion of India's civilizational heritage.

YOGA ON GLOBAL STAGE

Yet another notable endeavour of Prime Minister Modi has been the promotion of yoga on the global stage, with the United Nations declaring 21 June as International Yoga day. Modi has not only revived interest in India's holistic traditions, but also showcased its soft power to the world.

Modi in America doing yoga

ARTICLE 370

The abrogation of Article 370 by the Modi government marked a historic and transformative step towards the integration of Jammu and Kashmir into the mainstream of India. This bold move brought about a more unified and cohesive vision for the entire nation, ensuring equal rights and opportunities for the people of Jammu and Kashmir. It has opened avenues for development, economic growth, and improved governance in the region. The decision has also paved the way for greater inclusivity and connectivity, fostering a sense of national unity and solidarity.

Modi regarded the Supreme Court decision to uphold the scrapping of the Article 370 as a historic validation. The momentous ruling was seen by him as a beacon of hope, progress, and unity for the people of Jammu and Kashmir and Ladakh. With sagacity, the Court safeguarded the cherished essence of unity, a value deeply revered by the citizens of India. Prime Minister Modi assured the patient residents of Jammu and Kashmir and Ladakh that his government's unwavering commitment persisted in realising their dreams.

TRIPLE TALAQ

Triple *talaq* was another Supreme Court ruling that was highly contested and controversial in media and public, but had an overall positive effect on the lives of Muslim women who had been oppressed by the regressive religious law. On 22 August 2017, the Indian Supreme Court deemed instant triple *talaq (talaq-e-biddah)* unconstitutional.

On 30 July 2019, Parliament of India declared the practice of Triple *Talaq* illegal and unconstitutional and made it a punishable act from 1 August 2019.

Prime Minister Modi welcomed the judgement by the Supreme Court, calling it historic. He added that it would be a step forward for women empowerment in the country.

COVID-19

The Covid-19 pandemic was perhaps the most testing period of Prime Minister Modi's tenure. The respiratory illness claimed lives of millions across the globe. The Modi government demonstrated strong leadership and decisive actions to navigate the nation through unprecedented circumstances.

In March 2020, PM Modi announced a nationwide lockdown, one of the strictest in the world, to stop the spread of the virus. The decision while necessary for public health also posed some challenges for the economically vulnerable sections of the society. Modi's government, however, initiated various relief measures, including financial aid packages and free food distribution, to alleviate the hardships faced by millions of Indians.

Despite the challenges, the Modi government's efforts reflected resilience, adaptability, and a dedication to safeguard the well-being of the Indian populace.

Modi focused on ramping up India's healthcare infrastructure, increasing testing capabilities, and accelerating the vaccination drive. Under his leadership, India developed and distributed indigenous vaccines, such as Covaxin and Covisheild, contributing significantly to the global fight against Covid-19. On 30 January 2022, India announced that it had administered around 1.7 billion doses of vaccines and more than 720 million people were fully vaccinated.

The "Atmanirbhar Bharat" (self-reliant India) initiative was introduced to bolster the economy and support local businesses.

The government's communication strategies aimed at creating awareness and promoting

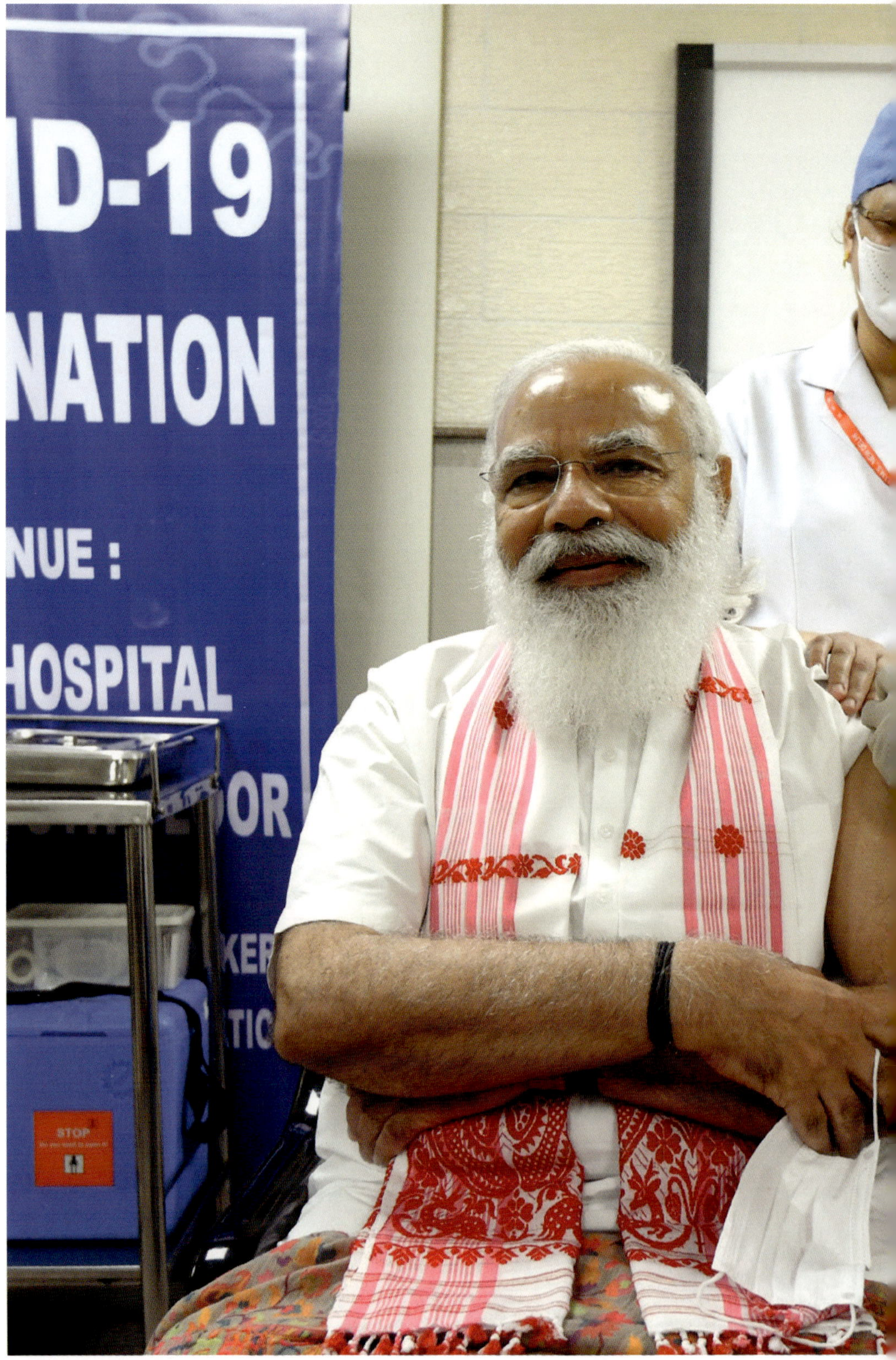

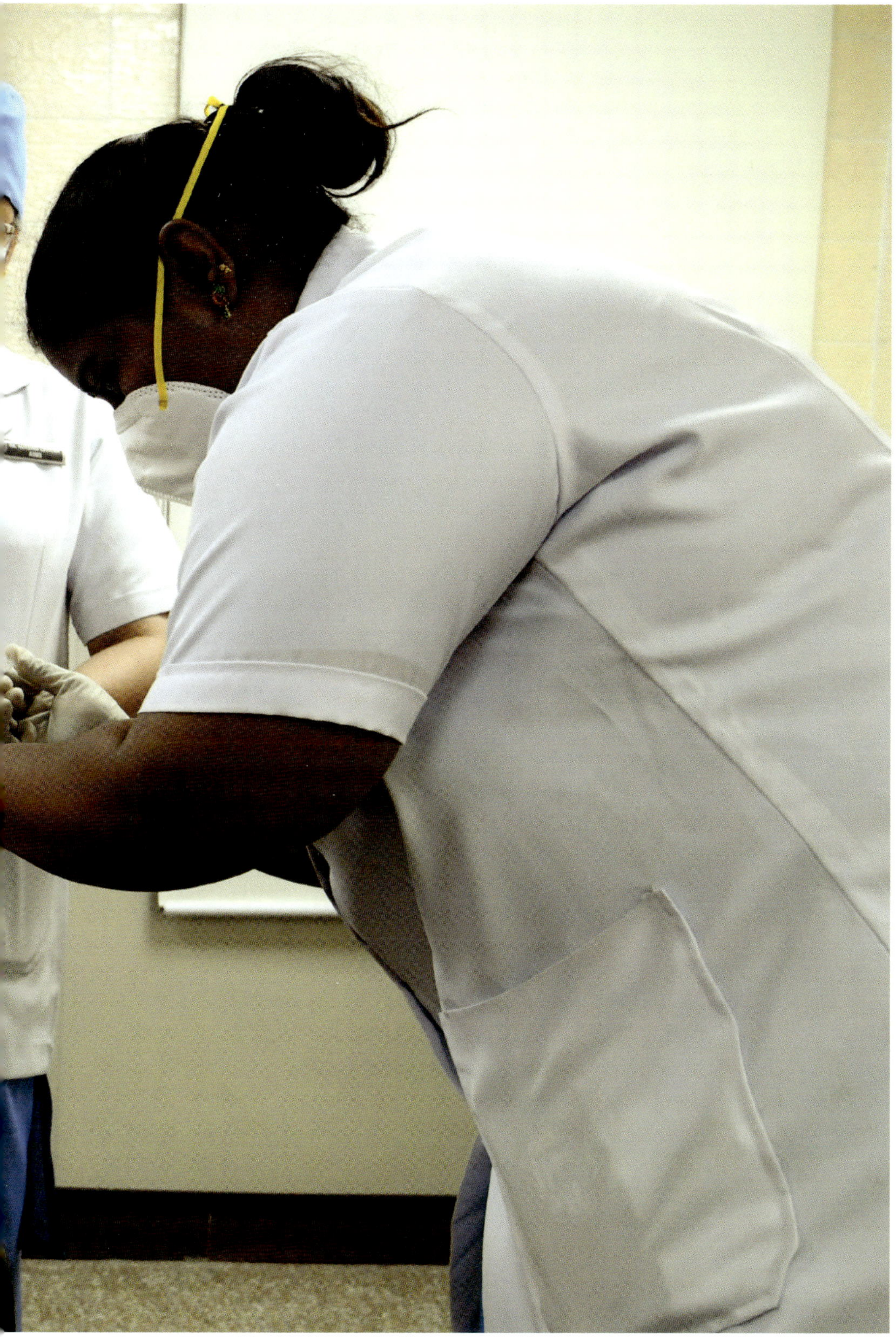

responsible behaviour played a crucial role in managing the crisis. Additionally, the collaborative approach with states and the international community showcased a commitment to a united front against the pandemic.

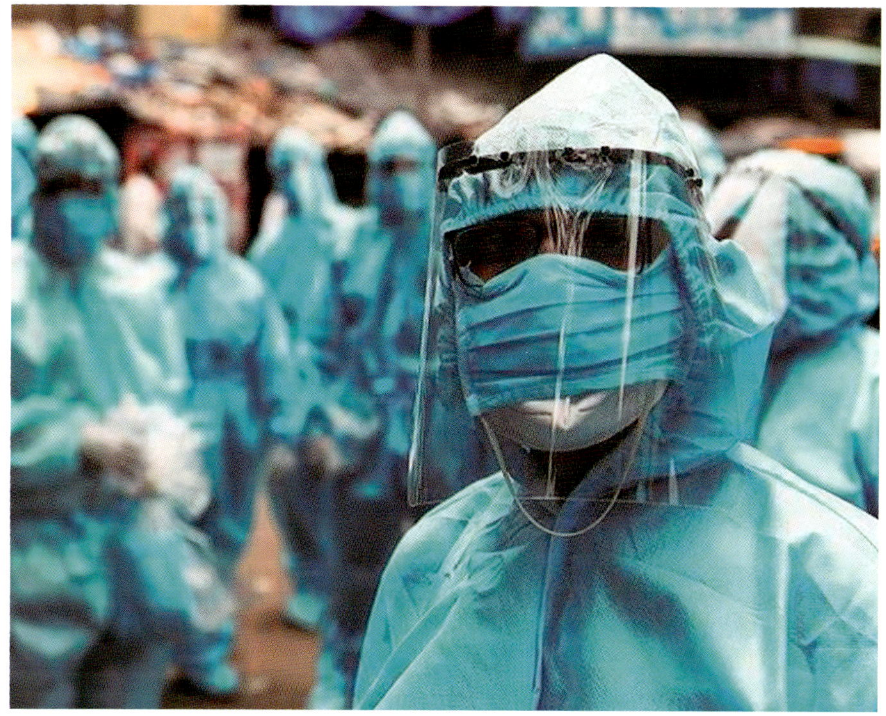

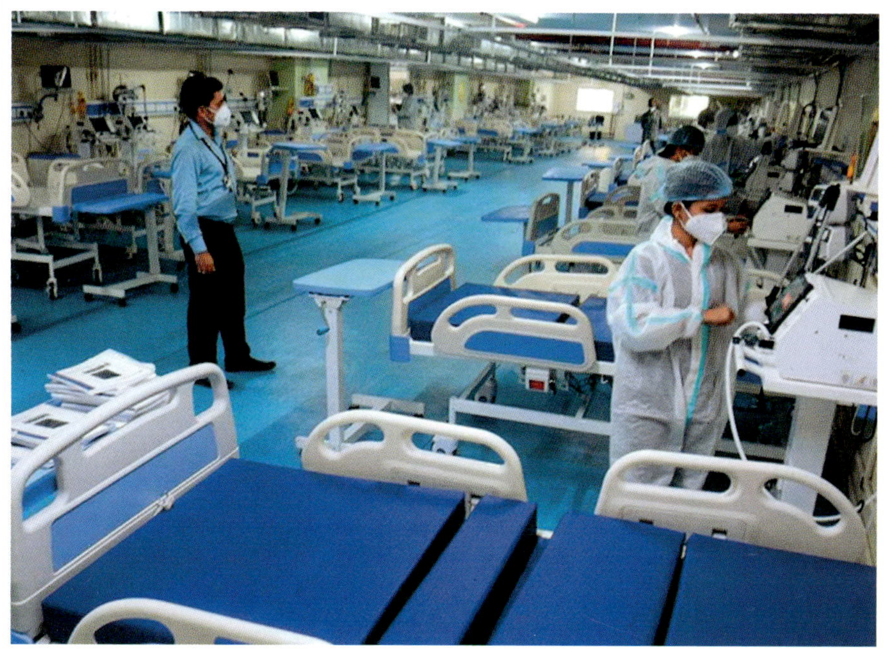

The violent practice of stone pelting in Kashmir has ceased

DEMONETISATION

Narendra Modi's decision to implement demonetisation in November 2016 was a bold and controversial move aimed at tackling corruption, black money, and counterfeit currency in India. The demonetisation policy involved the sudden invalidation of Rs 500 and Rs 1000 banknotes, which accounted for around 86 per cent of the country's currency in circulation at the time.

Despite some hardships and criticism, most people supported the initiative and believed it was a decisive step towards cleaning up the Indian economy. They agreed that it would curb the flow of illicit funds, disrupt terrorist financing networks, and promote digital transactions, thereby modernising India's financial infrastructure. Additionally, supporters believed that demonetisation would lead to long-term benefits such as increased tax compliance and a shift towards a more transparent economy.

GLOBAL SENSATION

AS THE Prime Minister was seen committed to address the domestic challenges, his international tours garnered global attention. His popularity soared to unprecedented levels as world leaders eagerly anticipated the chance to host him. Particularly noteworthy was a strong bond he developed with former US President Barack Obama.

Modi has forged a strong emotional chord with the Indian diaspora in the west. His visits are marked by enthusiastic receptions, with crowds cheering and showing immense respect for him. The level of adulation and respect he garners among people of Indian origin is something that would make any leader envious.

Ever since he assumed the office of Prime Minister, Modi has embarked on a remarkable journey, visiting more than 72 countries around the world and establishing close personal relations with leaders from many influential nations. He has made eight visits to the United States, seven to France, six to Germany, three to the UK and two visits to

Australia. His diplomacy extends to the G7 developed countries.

One unforgettable moment etched in history is the rock-star reception he received at New York's Madison Square Garden in September 2014. Non-resident Indians from across the United States came together in Modi's honour. It sent a resounding message to the world that India had arrived on the global stage.

In September 2019, the exuberant reception he received at the the "Howdy Modi" community summit held at NRG Stadium at Houston, Texas left an indelible mark as even then US President Donald Trump was visibly moved by the overwhelming response. Modi, leading the way, and Trump spontaneously taking a victory lap, much to the delight of the audience, in a moment that was entirely unplanned.

The camaraderie between Modi and Trump, as well as the growing closeness between India and the United States, was evident to all. Trump even went as far as likening Modi's popularity to that of the legendary king of pop, Elvis Presley, a testament to the Prime Minister's widespread appeal.

PM Modi with US President Donald Trump and his wife Melania Trump

This was repeated and outmatched at Modi's next historic visit to the US in 2023. The four-day visit was marked by ceremonial welcome, productive bilateral meetings with US President Joe Biden, a memorable address to a Joint Session of the US Congress, and engaging interactions with CEOs of top business corporations.

Earlier, Modi had the privilege of commemorating the ninth edition of International Yoga Day at the UN headquarters in New York, adding another significant event to his list of accomplishments on the global stage.

Critics speculated that Modi's rapport with Trump might pose a challenge in building a productive relationship with the newly elected US President Joe Biden. However, the sceptics were in for a surprise, as Indo-US relations continued to scale new heights. This was despite jarring notes that came due to the US expectations on Ukraine crisis and India's independent stand vis a vis Russia. Modi's dynamism and the shared imperative of managing China's influence have kept Indo-US relations on a positive trajectory. India has been forthright in asserting its commitment to not engage in bloc politics and to maintain independent relationships with other nations. The approach underscores India's resolve to pursue its national interests while fostering constructive partnerships globally.

Modi with US President Joe Biden

Addressing the US Parliament in June 2023, Prime Minister Modi said, 'the past few years, there have been many advances in AI – Artificial Intelligence. At the same time, there have been even more momentous developments in another AI – America and India'

(Left) PM Modi with Russian President Vladimir Putin, (Right) Aerospaces' F414 fighter-plane Engines

Despite reservations about India's choices such as its decision to import oil and maintain military ties with Russia, the United States has come to recognise the vital importance of a robust India in shaping a new global order.

Interestingly, Modi's positive relationship with Russian President Vladimir Putin has presented the world with avenue for discreet diplomacy with Russia. This backdoor channel could prove invaluable in facilitating international dialogue and cooperation with Russia, even in the face of differing stances on various issues. This explains why Biden went above and beyond the usual protocol to establish a personal connection with Modi. He hosted a state-dinner and both he and his wife Jill Biden engaged with Modi at numerous events. They hosted a private meal for the Indian Prime Minister, a rare honour!

The new evolving equation between the US and India was evident when India's HAL signed an agreement with GE of the US for joint production of Aerospaces' F414 fighter-plane Engines in India.

Modi's three-day visit to the US in September 2024 continued to demonstrate India's strong visibility at the global stage. As is customary now, the US held a super-show in Modi's honour, titled 'Modi and US.' Popular artists like music composer Devi Sri Prasad, rapper Hanumankind, and singer Aditya Gadhvi performed in the presence of over 13,500 diaspora audience at the Nassau Coliseum, New York.

Modi's visit to the United Kingdom in November 2015 will always be remembered for his historic reception at the famous Wembley Stadium in London where more than 60,000 people had gathered to hear him speak. The then Prime Minister of UK David Cameron made a prophetic declaration to the enthusiastic crowd: 'Team India, team UK – together we are a winning combination.' As the crowd erupted in cheers, he said it won't be long before Downing Street saw a British Indian Prime Minister.

Seven years later, in October 2022, Rishi Sunak, a British-born person of Indian origin, assumed the role of Prime Minister in the UK, making a historic milestone as the first Hindu to hold the prestigious position. The instant rapport and camaraderie between Prime Minister Modi and Prime Minister Sunak have paved the way for strengthening India-UK relations, promising a more robust partnership between the two nations.

Modi with Prime Minister of UK Rishi Sunak

Modi with French President Emmanuel Macron

India and France have enjoyed a long-lasting friendship, and this relationship experienced further consolidation during Modi's leadership. His notable visit to France, Germany and Canada in 2015 marked a significant moment in strengthening of ties between these nations.

During the time India and France joined forces to establish the International Solar Alliance, a pivotal initiative aimed at promoting the use of non-conventional sources of energy with the overarching goal of contributing to global sustainability and combating climate change.

India solidified its defence ties with France through significant agreements, including the procurement of 36 Rafale aircraft for the Indian Air Force and the acquisition of three submarines along with other defence technology collaborators.

France also committed to participate in India's 'Make in India' mission, emphasising its role as a trusted partner.

France delivered the first batch of five Rafale aircraft to India in July 2020. This timely delivery occurred just two months after Chinese aggression in the Galwan Valley, underlining the importance of bolstering India's defence capabilities.

During Modi's visit to Paris in July 2023, India further expanded its defence cooperation with France by signing agreements for the acquisition of 26 Rafale aircraft for the Indian Navy, along with three submarines. The reinforced collaboration exemplifies the strong ties between the two nations.

Modi had previously established a close personal

rapport with French President Emmanuel Jean Michel Frederic Macron, which has been instrumental in fostering these strategic partnerships. France has also supported India's rightful claim for a permanent seat on the UN Security Council, underscoring the depth of their diplomatic relations.

Canada is India's ninth largest trading partner. Prime Minister Modi's visit to Canada in April 2015 elevated the bilateral relation to a strategic partnership. Both the counties signed agreements related to Patents, Nuclear Cooperation, Agriculture, an Extradition Treaty, Mutual Legal Assistance Treaty, Agreement on Cooperation in Agriculture, Science and Technology and Environment Cooperation and Energy cooperation.

Modi unveils statue of Mahtma Gandhi in Hannover

Together with German Chancellor Angela Merkel, Modi inaugurated the world's largest industrial fare in Hanover in April 2015. He also unveiled the statue of Mahatma Gandhi. Modi said that Indian Lions and German Eagles were great partners.

Germany lost the fighter jet deal to France but emerged a strong contender to build six Non-Nuclear military submarines for India costing Rs 43,000 Crore. The prestigious P-751 India (India Submarine Acquisition Project) is one of the biggest 'Make in India' programmes under which manufacturing would take place in India in collaboration with the strategic partners.

During his three-day visit to Australia in November 2014, Modi made history by becoming the first Indian Prime Minister to address a joint sitting of both Houses of the Australian Federal

Modi with Prime Minister of Australia Tony Abbott

Parliament. This visit followed a significant diplomatic exchange, as two months earlier, Australian Prime Minister Tony Abbott had visited India. These meetings were set against the backdrop of G20 Summit held in Brisbane, where leaders converged to discuss matters of economic and strategic cooperation.

When Modi returned to Australia in 2023, after a nine-year gap, he received a hero's welcome. The Indian diaspora had meticulously organised a grand reception for him at the Qudos Bank Arena Stadium in Sydney. Thousands of people in attendance continuously applauded during

an hour-long speech, exemplifying the remarkable soft power that India had come to represent. The newly appointed Australian Prime Minister, Antony Albanese, who had assumed office in 2022, was visibly impressed by the reception that the Indian Prime Minister received, further cementing the strong rapport between the two nations.

Modi has cultivated new and trusted friends but not at the cost of old ones. Among these enduring friendships, the bond between India and Russia, particularly with President Vladimir Putin at the helm, remains robust and dependable. Collaborations between the two nations extend to defence, energy resources, Nuclear technology, and space exploration. Russia is already supplying S-400 air defence missile system that is poised to safeguard Indian airspace, effectively preventing any hostile aircraft or missile from penetrating within the range of up to 400 kilometers.

India has always stood by Russia as an unwavering friend, demonstrating steadfast support. It refrained from voting against Russian aggression in Ukraine even as it advocated dialogue as a way to resolve conflict.

Narendra Modi has declared time and again that the era of war is over and dialogue is the only way to resolve conflict. Even when the UN demanded that Russia should reverse its annexation of Ukraine, India abstained from voting. It abstained even when a UN resolution condemned Russian invasion on Ukraine.

Prime Minister Modi has on numerous occasions reiterated that the age of war has passed, emphasising the paramount importance of dialogue in resolving conflicts. Even when the United Nations called for Russia to reverse its annexation of Ukraine, India maintained a stance of abstention, underscoring its commitment to a diplomatic approach.

India chose not to align itself with western and European nations in imposing sanctions against Russia. Instead, it opted to maintain bilateral relations, charting its own diplomatic course. It continued to uphold separate arrangements for importing oil from Russia, even in the face of disapproval from the United States and other countries. This approach underscores India's commitment to pursue its national interests and foreign policy objectives independently.

Rather than isolating, the Indian Prime Minister believes in engaging with Russia more intensely. Putin calls him a big friend of Russia. They share a wonderful relation of mutual trust. The US, the West and Europe have started respecting the Indian position. Now they know that they have someone they can approach if they want to reach Putin.

PM Modi visited Russia on July 8, 2024, on a personal invitation by President Vladimir Putin. He was also awarded Russia's highest civilian award, Order of Saint Andrew the Apostle, during his visit. The two world leaders held discussions on defense and trade deals to facilitate further increase in trade and joint investment projects between the far East region of Russia and India.

Prime Minister Narendra Modi visited Ukraine on August 23 on the invitation of President Volodymyr Zelenskyy. This was the first visit of an Indian PM to Ukraine since the country gained independence in 1991. Modi and Zelenskyy visited a memorial for hundreds of children who have died in the war between Ukraine and Russia. Modi remarked that killing of children in war was unacceptable and that he'd come to Ukraine with a plea for peace.

(second from left) PM Modi at the 12th East Asia Summit

The way Modi has built a circle of friends in the Pacific is laudable. The QUAD (Quadrilateral Security Dialogue), which is strategic alliance of Australia, Japan, the USA and India is significant for the Pacific. At the ASEAN summit in Manila in 2017, Shinzo Abe of Japan, Malcolm Turnbull of Australia, Donald Trump of the US and Narendra Modi decided to revive the grouping to counter China's growing assertiveness in the Pacific.

India has significantly strengthened its links with South East Asia, particularly with the nations like Vietnam, the Philippines and Indonesia. Under the leadership of Narendra Modi, the Look East Policy has evolved into the Act East Policy. Modi has made dedicated efforts to strengthen these diplomatic ties. En route to China for the G20 summit in September 2016, he visited Vietnam for two days. This was the first visit by an Indian Prime Minister in 15 years.

India and Vietnam are already involved in strategic defence deals. India is cooperating with Vietnam in exploration of oil and natural gas. Vietnam with its old cultural links with India is a champion of free navigation and maritime security.

During Modi's visit, twelve agreements were signed. The relationship was upgraded from 'strategic partnership' to 'comprehensive strategic partnership.' This opened new possibilities. The visit focused on enhanced defence cooperation which is significant since India too has strategic interest in South China Sea.

In 2017, Prime Minister Modi made a trip to Manila to participate in the ASEAN India summit and the East Asia summit. The focal point of discussions on the first day of the summit was the South China Sea dispute, highlighting the concerns of ASEAN nations regarding China's assertive actions in the region.

During his address to the Indian community gathered there, Modi conveyed a clear message, emphasising India's principled stance. He affirmed that India has always been a nation that does not seek to take what belongs to others, underlining India's commitment to peaceful co-existence and respect for sovereignty.

(Left) PM Modi with Singaporean PM Lawrence Wong and (Right) with Hassanal Bolkiah, PM of Brunei

At Bali (Indonesia), in November 2022, when G20 Presidency was handed over to India, Modi said: 'India will assume the G-20 Presidency for the coming year. Our agenda will be inclusive, ambitious, decisive and action-oriented. We will work to realise all aspects of our vision of 'One Earth, One Family, One Future'.

PM Modi's visits to Singapore and Brunei in September marked the first-ever visit by an Indian Prime Minister to these countries.

Prime Minister Modi arrived in Bandar Seri Begawan in Brunei on an official visit on September 3 at the invitation of Sultan Haji Hassanal Bolkiah. The historic visit of the Prime Minister coincided with the 40th anniversary of establishment of diplomatic ties between India and Brunei. Yet again, Modi opened new, hitherto closed off paths of negotiation with countries that have long been in India's vicinity but always out of reach of other leaders.

Ever since he became the Prime Minister, Narendra Modi has demonstrated a 'neighbour-first approach' in his foreign policy. He recognises the fact that neighbours cannot be changed and it is essential to have strong and good relations with them. Notably, his administration successfully resolved the long-drawn-out boundary dispute with Bangladesh through the exchange of enclaves, a significant diplomatic achievement.

'Sometimes we wonder if there can be solutions to problems with neighbours.There was a land dispute with Bangladesh ever since that country was born in 1971. The question was pending. One issue was about water sharing, another about demarcation of boundary in the sea and third about the land boundary,' Modi pointed out while addressing a gathering of Indian diaspora in Brussels in May 2016.

The historic agreement for exchange of enclaves with Bangladesh was achieved in 2015 and the agreement was signed in Dhaka between Modi and Bangladesh Prime Minister Sheikh Hasina on 6 June 2015. Under the land boundary agreement, the dispute over 162 enclaves was amicably settled. Both the countries pledged to root out terrorism and India gave Bangladesh USD 2 billion line of credit.

Modi visited Dacca again in 2021 when three major events coincided: It was the Golden Jubilee of the Independence of Bangladesh, the birth centenary of Sheikh Mujibur Rahman, the father of the nation of Bangladesh, and 50 years of establishment of diplomatic relations between India and Bangladesh.

During his visit, Prime Minister Modi awarded the 2020 Gandhi Peace Prize to Sheikh Mujibur Rehman, a significant milestone as it marked the first posthumus presentation of the prestigious award. Sheikh Mujibur Rehman's daughters Sheikh Hasina and Sheikh Rehana graciously accepted the award on his behalf.

The visit also witnessed both countries jointly deciding to celebrate and strengthen their bilateral relations. India announced the establishment of the Bangladesh Chair at Delhi University, further cementing ties between the nations. Additionally, India pledged to provide 1000 Shuborno Jayanti scholarships to Bangladeshi students pursuing their studies in India.

The high point of the meeting was Modi's visit to Jessoreshwari temple in Shyamnagar of Satkshira district and the other to the birthplace of the Matua gurus, Harichand and Guruchand, in Orakandi.

Modi performing Pooja at the Jeshoreshwari Kali Temple, in Satkhira, Bangladesh on March 27, 2021

PM Modi with Bhutan's PM Lotay Tshering

Modi with Bhutan's King, Jigme Khesar Namgyel Wangchuck

Modi's love and respect for India's immediate Himalayan neighbour was evident when he visited Bhutan in June 2014. This was Modi's first visit outside India and the way people lined up on both sides of the road in Thimphu demonstrated the love people of Bhutan have for the country. The visit was also a manifestation of Modi's 'neighbour-first' policy.

'India is associated with the progress and happiness of Bhutan and will continue to be. The two countries are made for each other. The colour of our passports may vary, but our heritage and values remain the same', he said during a royal banquet.

In 2019, Modi visited Bhutan again to preside over the inauguration of the Supreme Court building project constructed with India's assistance. During his visit, both nations sealed deals on 10 crucial Memorandums of Understandings (MoUs), covering diverse areas such as telecom, space, education and power.

Reflecting on the strong ties between the two nations, Modi said, 'India is honoured to have a friend and a neighbour like Bhutan and we take pride in contributing to the development and progress of Bhutan.

Modi with Nepali PM KP Sharma Oli

Modi visited Nepal in August 2014. This was the first time in 17 years that an Indian Prime Minister had visited the country. The visit aimed to acknowledge and honour the deep cultural and historical ties that bind India and Nepal while reaffirming India's unwavering commitment to its neighbouring nations.

'This is the land of *Sita* and *Janak*, and Nepal-India ties are as ancient as the Himalayas and the Ganga,' he said. He emphasised the paramount importance of the chemistry between the two countries. 'My visit underscores the richness of our shared heritage, encompassing nature, history, culture, spiritualism and religion. We are committed to nurturing our relations with Nepal to elevating our partnership to new heights,' he said. While addressing the Nepalese Parliament, Modi announced Rs 10,000 crore concessional credit to Nepal. He proposed a HIT formula for development where H means Highways, I means Information Highways and T means Transways. 'These three when combined together would pave the way for rapid development of the country and India wants to give this gift to our neighbour at the earliest,' he said.

In November, same year, Modi visited Nepal again, this time to attend the 18th SAARC Summit. The bilateral meeting and the response Modi received from the people indicated that he had established a rapport that India and Nepal had not experienced before. Doubts were replaced with trust, and mere platitudes gave way to concrete actions. India delivered a state-of-art trauma centre to Nepal and presented the Nepalese army with a versatile multipurpose helicopter. Numerous agreements were signed to solidify India's commitment to advancing Nepal's development. A new cross-border bus service known as Pashupatinath Express, was inaugurated to enhance connectivity between the two nations. That Modi visited Nepal five times in last 10 years is a testament to his attempts to create a special equation with neighbouring countries. India also played an active role in the efforts to promote peace and stability in Afghanistan, especially in light of the US withdrawal. At the G20 Summit on Afghanistan, Modi voiced India's concerns, with a particular emphasis on preventing Afghan territory from becoming a breeding ground for radicalisation and terrorism.

SAARC
he 18th SAARC Summit
Kathmandu, Nepal
26-27 November 2014
Bhutan
India
Chairperson
Nepal
Maldives
Pakistan
Sri Lanka

G20
भारत 2023 INDIA
वसुधैव कुटुम्बकम्
ONE EARTH • ONE FAMILY • ONE FUTUR
INDONESIA
BHARAT
BRAZIL

PM Modi and President of India, Droupadi Murmu with G20 foreign leaders

वसुधैव कुटुम्बकम्
ONE EARTH
ONE FAMILY • ONE FUTURE

G20
भारत 2023 INDIA
वसुधैव कुटुम्बकम्
ONE EARTH
ONE FAMILY • ONE FUTURE

वसुधैव कुटुम्बकम्
ONE EARTH
ONE FAMILY • ONE FUTURE

वसुधैव कुटुम्बकम्
ONE EARTH

G20
भारत 2023 INDIA
वसुधैव कुटुम्बकम्
ONE EARTH
ONE FAMILY • ONE FUTURE

2023 INDIA
वसुधैव कुटुम्बकम्
ONE EARTH

वसुधैव कुटुम्बकम्
ONE EARTH

वसुधैव कुटुम्बकम
ONE EARTH
ONE FAMILY • ONE FUTURE
INDIA

G20
भारत 2023 INDIA
वसुधैव कुटुम्बकम
ONE EARTH
ONE FAMILY • ONE FUTURE

2023 INDIA
वसुधैव कुटुम्बकम
ONE EARTH
ONE FAMILY • ONE FUTURE

INDIA

G20
भारत 2023 INDIA
वसुधैव कुटुम्बकम
ONE EARTH
ONE FAMILY • ONE FUTURE

INDIA

INDIA

G20
भारत 2023 INDIA
वसुधैव कुटुम्बकम
ONE EARTH
ONE FAMILY • ONE FUTURE

INDIA
वसुधैव कुटुम्बकम
ONE EARTH
ONE FAMILY • ONE FUTURE

ONE FAMILY

G20
भारत 2023 INDIA
ONE EARTH

G20
भारत 2023 INDIA

ONE FAMILY

G20
भारत 2023 INDIA
वसुधैव कुटुम्बकम
ONE EARTH

G20
भारत 2023 INDIA
ONE EARTH

वसुधैव कुटुम्बकम
ONE EARTH

G20
भारत 2023 INDIA
ONE EARTH

G20
भारत 2023 INDIA

वसुधैव कुटुम्बकम्
ONE EARTH
2023 INDIA

ONE FAMILY • ONE

ONE FAMILY • ONE

ONE FAMILY • ONE

2023 INDIA

वसुधैव कुटुम्बकम्
ONE EARTH
ONE FAMILY • ONE FUTURE
2023 INDIA

ONE FAMILY • ONE

ONE FAMILY • ONE

THE VIBGYOR THAT IS MODI

SPIRITUAL MODI

SPIRITUAL MODI, as a child would often sit in the tin shed at Vadnagar railway station talking for hours into the day with wandering sadhus. He wanted to know everything - how they lived, what was their calling, and where they would go from there? The sadhus indulged him, drinking his tea and answering the questions of the young inquisitive child. Vadnagar has strong traces of Buddhism.

Chinese pilgrim Hieun Tsang visited Vadnagar and described the existence of monasteries and hostels for monks. Buddhism has had a strong influence on Modi's life. He had read extensively about Buddhism and would try to find meaning in renunciation. When he left home and family in that search, there was resistance from all his relatives, especially his mother, but finally Modi succeeded in persuading them. During his teens he went to the Himalayas, Vivekananda Ashram at Belur Math, and was convinced that he wanted to become a Sadhu.

Later, when he returned home to a normal life he would still spend his Diwali alone at some secluded place. He still believes in interacting with one's inner self once in a while. Spending days alone in the Gir forests, all he would carry in the *jhola* (clothed bag) that hung from his shoulder was a pair of clothes and few eatables to survive. Modi has the makings of a mendicant in him. It is unusual to find a man in public life with such deep-rooted spiritualism. For years he would systematically burn his belongings that were not necessary to survive as he felt that they created attachment. 'People should remember me by my work and not through things,' he told one of his friends. Everything that existed would eventually vanish and burning things was his way of disconnecting with his past.

PM Modi with Dalai Lama

TO YOU, I BOW

MODI HAS always been known as a person of immense humility and compassion. Trained in the RSS, respect for elders is ingrained in his character. When it came to seeking the blessings of senior leaders of the party and the RSS in the time-old Indian tradition of touching their feet, Modi has never fallen short. While people such as Keshubhai bitterly opposed him, he did not allow political rivalry to spoil the personal relation. Every time he became the Chief Minister, he touched Keshubhai's feet to seek his blessings.

The *guru-shishya* tradition is rooted in our psyche and Modi is a staunch believer in it. While inaugurating a computer lab in Vadnagar as the CM of Gujarat, he politely declined to be garlanded by any of his teachers. Instead, he invited them all to his old classroom and feted each one of them. It is his belief that no matter where he reaches in life, he will remain a student and his teacher, a figure of reverence.

JAI HIND

PRIME MINISTER Narendra Modi has always felt a strong affinity for the Indian Army, which he has demonstrated through various actions throughout his life. As a young man, he couldn't afford to attend the Sainik School in Balachadi, but his admiration for the army led him to serve tea to soldiers passing through Mehsana railway station, a gesture of respect for their dedication to the nation.

His connection with the army deepened further during his tenure in the Haryana when he ensured that a Lok Sabha ticket was given to Sudha Yadav, a Kargil war widow, showcasing his empathy and support for military families.

Modi's visit to the icy terrain of Siachen to meet with the brave soldiers stationed there exemplify his unwavering commitment to the armed forces. This high-altitude region, known as the world's highest battlefield, holds strategic significance for India. Despite the harsh conditions, soldiers endure extreme cold and tough terrain to safeguard the nation's borders.

During his visit, PM Modi expressed gratitude to the soldiers for their unwavering dedication and sacrifice. He emphasised the nation's support and appreciation for their service, acknowledging the immense challenges they face in guarding the frontier. Modi's presence not only boosted the morale of the soldiers but also highlighted the government's commitment to their well-being.

Furthermore, PM Modi reviewed the operational preparedness and infrastructure development in the region. He was briefed on the various measures taken to enhance the living and working conditions of the soldiers, including the provision of better clothing, equipment, and medical facilities. He also expressed his concern for the environment, highlighting the need to minimise the ecological impact of military activities in the region.

PM Modi's visit to Siachen is a testament to his unwavering support for the armed forces and his commitment to their welfare. It sends a strong message to the nation and the world that India is determined to protect its borders and maintain its territorial integrity, no matter how challenging the circumstances.

VALIANT OFFICERS OF 122 AIR FORCE SQUADRON

Prime Minister Narendra Modi's decision to celebrate Diwali with security forces in Lepcha, Himachal Pradesh in 2023 reflects his deep appreciation for their service and sacrifice. Donning a camouflage jacket, PM Modi spent quality time with the personnel, underscoring the significance of their contributions to national security. This gesture not only acknowledges their relentless dedication but also uplifts their spirits, particularly during festive occasions when they are away from their families.

Under Modi's leadership, the long-standing demand for the One Rank, One Pension (OROP) scheme was fulfilled in 2015, ensuring uniform pension payments for retired armed forces personnel. This scheme aimed to ensure uniform pension payments for armed forces personnel retiring in the same rank with the same length of service, regardless of their retirement date. Implemented in 2015, the OROP scheme addressed disparities in pension benefits among retired military personnel, providing them with fair and equitable treatment.

Prime Minister Modi's government took proactive steps to fulfill this promise, recognising the sacrifices and contributions of the armed forces to the nation's security. By resolving the OROP issue, the government demonstrated its commitment to the welfare and well-being of military vetrans. This initiative not only rectified disparities in pension benefits but also boosted the morale of retired personnel, reaffirming the government's commitment to their welfare.

Spearheaded under Modi government, The Agnipath Scheme, focuses to prepare young men and women for a career in the armed forces by providing comprehensive training. In his address to the first batch of *Agniveers* via video conferencing, Modi emphasised the values of discipline, dedication, and determination, underlining the importance of these qualities in the life of a soldier. A path-breaking initiative launched by the Indian government aims to provide comprehensive training to the youth of the country, equipping them with the necessary skills and knowledge to serve the nation with pride and honour.

From his humble beginnings serving tea to soldiers to his efforts in ensuring the welfare of military families and implementing crucial schemes like One Rank, One Pension, Modi has consistently demonstrated his unwavering commitment to those who serve the nation.

ANIMAL FARM

MODI HAS been enamoured with animals and birds since he was a child. When he was just 13 years old, he carried a baby crocodile home. The croc had been lying on the banks of the Sharmishtha Lake where he used to go for a swim daily early in the morning. He thought the croc was unwell and needed love. Heeraba promptly asked him to take it back. Obediently but reluctantly, Modi dropped the croc back near the lake.

Once he was hit very hard by the tail of one of the crocs that led to nine stitches on his left foot near the ankle and confinement in bed for more than a week. He still has those cut marks that look like he was struck with a sharp weapon. 'A crocodile's tail is very strong,' Modi says while describing this incident. Anybody else would have stopped going to the lake. But the young boy of Class VIII was not scared. Within a month he was back swimming in the lake. Even today all animals and birds, from dogs to peacocks or ducks in the PM house premises are treated with affection. At times when the PM is sitting in the lawn, he invites dogs and ducks to play with him.

Modi's commitment to environmental conservation is evident in his proactive approach to protecting India's biodiversity and natural heritage. By endorsing the Cheetah Reintroduction Project, he demonstrates his belief in the importance of preserving endangered species and restoring ecological balance. Modi's backing of the Cheetah Reintroduction Project aligns with his broader agenda of sustainable development and wildlife conservation.

By reintroducing the cheetah, he not only seeks to revive the population of this magnificent species but also aims to promote ecosystem health and biodiversity conservation in India's diverse landscapes.

Through initiatives like these, he envisions a future where India's rich biodiversity thrives, ensuring a sustainable and resilient environment for generations to come.

LEISURELY PLEASURES

AMIDST THE relentless demands of his schedule, Prime Minister Narendra Modi discovers moments of solace and renewal through his cherished leisurely pursuits. With unwavering dedication, Modi devotes time to activities that nourish his mind, body, and spirit.

Through the tranquil practices of reading, yoga, and photography, he not only finds respite from the pressures of his duties but also embodies the essence of balance and mindfulness in navigating life's myriad responsibilities.

Although not a foodie. Modi is adept at cooking various Gujarati dishes. As a child he used to feel deeply empathetic towards his hard working mother and would try to help her in cooking. His childhood meals were not lavish and he loved to eat *bajari no rotlo with cha* (tea). As a *Pracharak* Modi was not demanding in food and would eat whatever came his way. His favourite, however, was *handwo* (a gujarati dish). Now, as PM preferred food is *khichdi* with *kadhi* or milk. A simpler meal cannot be imagined.

Modi has been known for his distinctive fashion sense that often blends traditional Indian attire with modern styles. Modi's fashion choices have garnered attention both domestically and internationally.

One of the most iconic aspects of Modi's wardrobe is his preference for traditional Indian clothing, particularly the *kurta-pyjama* combination. He is often seen sporting vibrant-colored *kurtas* paired with crisp white *pajamas*, a look that reflects his cultural roots and resonates with many Indians.

This attire not only showcases his pride in Indian heritage but also presents a dignified yet accessible image to the public.

YOUTH ICON

OUR CHILDREN, OUR FUTURE

PRIME MINISTER Narendra Modi's connection with children transcends politics, reflecting a deep-seated commitment to nurturing the future of India through education and empowerment. Renowned for his genuine affection for young minds, Modi's interactions with children reveal a compassionate leader who sees immense potential in every child.

From his active participation in educational campaigns to his innovative initiatives aimed at fostering inclusive learning environments, Modi's approach to educating children embodies both pragmatism and empathy.

Central to Modi's commitment to education is the *Beti Bachao, Beti Padhao (BBBP)* initiative, which addresses the issue of gender disparity in education. By raising awareness about the importance of girls' education and providing financial incentives to families, BBBP aims to ensure that every girl has access to quality education and the opportunity to fulfill her potential.

Through initiatives like *Kanya Kelavani*, where girls are rewarded for school enrollment, Modi is working to break down barriers and create a more inclusive educational system.

Pariksha Pe Charcha is an annual event organised by the Government of India, where Prime Minister Narendra Modi interacts with students, teachers, and parents to address their concerns and queries related to exam stress and career choices. The event was first organised in 2018 and has since become a much-anticipated event for students across the country. In the 6th edition of *Pariksha Pe Charcha*, PM Modi shared insightful interactions with students, teachers, and parents at *Talkatora* Stadium in New Delhi.

The event also included a visit by the Prime Minister to witness the exhibits showcasing students' achievements before the interactive session commenced. *Pariksha Pe Charcha*, conceptualised by the Prime Minister himself, serves as a platform for open dialogue on various topics related to life and examinations.

Pariksha Pe
Charcha 2023

Mr. Kannamala Vamsi Krishna, Telangana

This year's edition of PPC witnessed an overwhelming response, with about **38.80 Lakh** registrations from **155 countries**. The significant participation reflects the growing importance and relevance of the initiative in addressing the concerns and aspirations of students, parents, and educators worldwide.

Under the leadership of Prime Minister Narendra Modi, the Government of India has implemented a range of scholarship programmes aimed at promoting education and fostering equal opportunities for students from diverse socio-economic backgrounds. These initiatives encompass schemes such as the National Means Cum-Merit Scholarship (NMMSS), which targets economically disadvantaged students in Classes 9 to 12, and the Post-Matric Scholarship Scheme for Minorities, offering support to minority community students pursuing higher education. Additionally, the government has launched the National Scholarship Portal (NSP), streamlining the application process and ensuring efficient disbursement of scholarships across various central and state schemes. These efforts reflect a commitment to empowering youth through education, addressing financial barriers, and fostering a more inclusive and equitable educational landscape in India.

The introduction of the National Education Policy (NEP) 2020, is a landmark reform aimed at making education in India more representative of Indian ethos and suitable for the country's future needs. The policy aims to transform education into a holistic, flexible, inclusive, multidisciplinary, and technology-oriented system.

It introduces a new 5+3+3+4 design for school education, which includes foundational years, preparatory years, middle years, and high school. The policy also promotes the use of technology in education, including online learning, artificial intelligence, and virtual labs.

Recently, PM Modi presented the first ever National creators awards to all the young people who have used their creative minds to bring positive change in the society. The Disruptor of the year award was given to Youtuber Ranbeer Allahbadia, who has used the platform to raise awareness about topics like sleep deprivation and other sensitive topics.

The Best Storyteller Award was given to Keerthika Govindhasamy, who teaches history to the people of India through her Youtube channel, Keerthi History.

Modi's attempts to interact and reward the youth of India shows his genuine interest in their progress and how he envisions them as the future of the country.

CREATORS
AWARD

AWARD

(from left) Kangana Ranaut, Aamir Khan, Shah Rukh Khan and PM Modi

SKILL INDIA

Under the visionary leadership of Prime Minister Narendra Modi, the Skill India campaign has emerged as a beacon of hope for millions of Indian youth seeking to unlock their full potential and contribute meaningfully to the nation's progress. Since its inception, Skill India has a range of transformative initiatives aimed at equipping individuals with the necessary skills to thrive in today's dynamic job market.

At the heart of the Skill India mission lies the Pradhan Mantri Kaushal Vikas Yojana (PMKVY), a pioneering scheme designed to provide vocational training to over 10 million youth across the country. By offering short-term skill development courses aligned with the National Skills Qualification Framework (NSQF), PMKVY has empowered countless individuals to acquire industry-relevant skills and secure gainful employment.

Skill India's impact extends beyond urban centers, with initiatives such as the Deen Dayal Upadhyaya Grameen Kaushalya Yojana (DDU-GKY) bringing skill development opportunities to rural communities.

JUKI

With projections indicating a surplus manpower of 4 to 5 crore over the next decade, the Prime Minister rightly highlights the urgency of providing this youthful workforce with the requisite skills. He aptly warns that without proper skill development, the demographic dividend could potentially turn into a challenge rather than an advantage.

The Prime Minister's call for elevating India's ITIs to global standards aligns with the contemporary need for skilled manpower across various industries. By emphasising the importance of constant updating of training programs and syllabi to align with evolving technology and industry requirements, he demonstrates a forward-looking approach towards skill development.

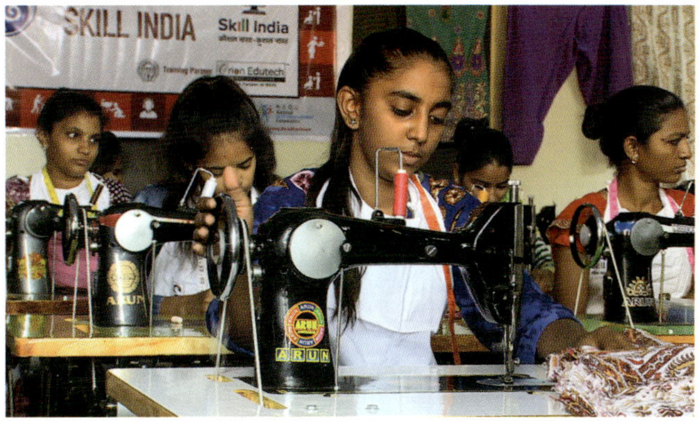

MORE SINNED AGAINST THAN SINNING

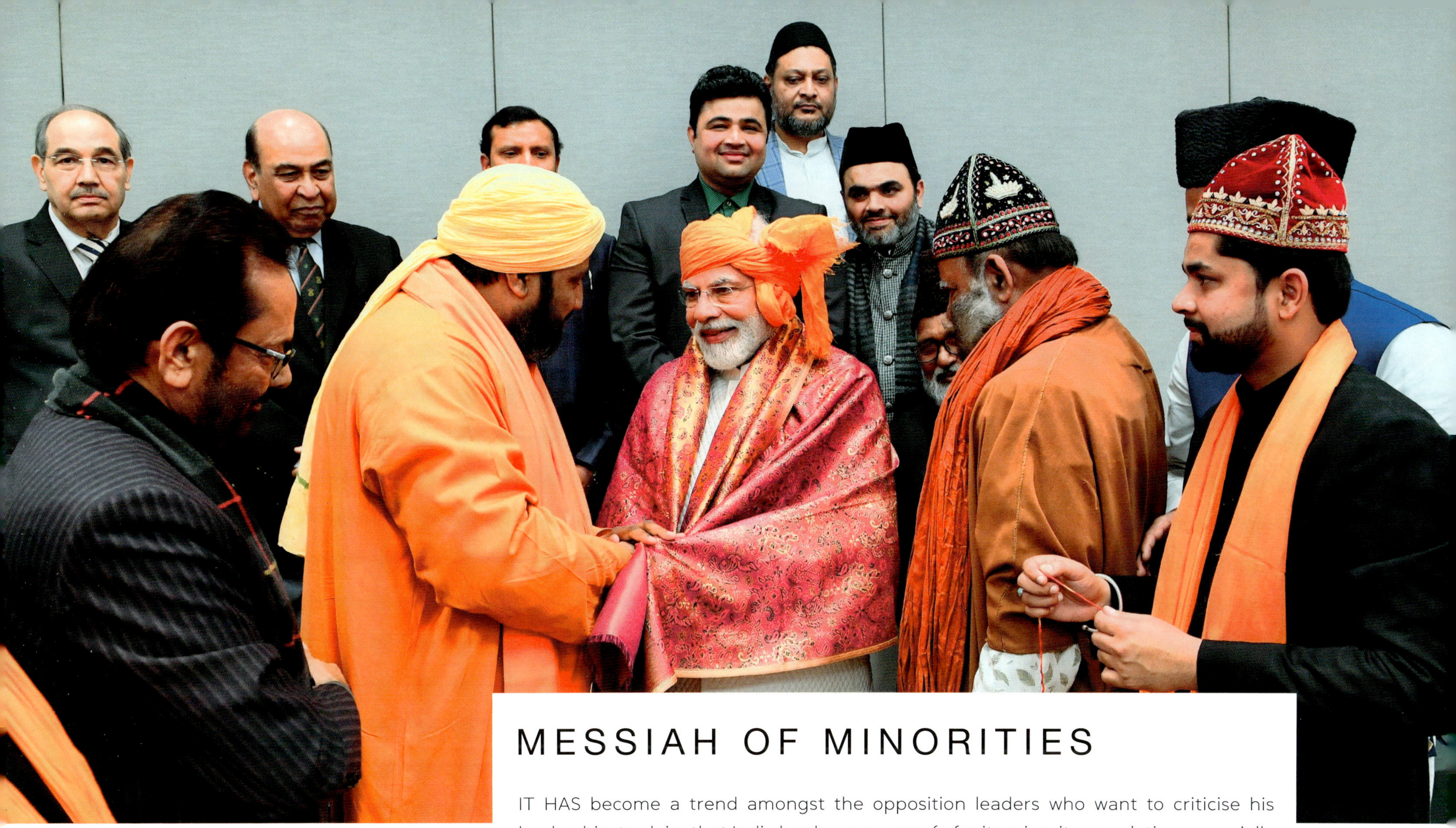

MESSIAH OF MINORITIES

IT HAS become a trend amongst the opposition leaders who want to criticise his leadership, to claim that India has become unsafe for its minority population, especially Muslims. But if we look at the hard facts and the ground reality, the widely perceived belief that Modi has an ambivalent relationship with Indian Muslims finds little proof. Modi grew up in Vadnagar's Kala Vasudev area which adjoins the Muslim locality of Sembhavada.

He spent his childhood playing with young Muslim boys and is remembered as always being courteous by Babubhai Amirbhai Khan or Babu *Chacha*, a tea seller. Growing up, Modi considered Muslims no different from Hindus. Modi's father had given shelter to a young Muslim boy Abbas Mohhammad Ramsada, who'd lost his father. Abbas still remembers how well and equally he was treated by the Modi family. With support and love, Abbas was able to complete his MCom and LLB and secured a position in the Gujarat government.

Schemes to uplift Muslim Community

Narendra Modi's leadership has seen a significant shift in addressing the concerns of marginalised sections within the Muslim community. Notably, his support for Muslim women during the Triple *Talaq* ban garnered widespread appreciation, signalling a commitment to gender equality and women's rights. Furthermore, Modi's advocacy for the *Pasmanda* Muslims, who have long been overlooked by mainstream political parties, reflects a dedication to addressing the needs of all segments of society, irrespective of religious affiliation. Unlike previous administrations, which often treated the Muslim community merely as a vote bank, Modi's BJP aims to integrate Muslims into the national mainstream, fostering inclusivity and unity.

The BJP's outreach to Sufis is emblematic of its broader strategy to engage with diverse Muslim groups and promote cultural pluralism. By extending efforts beyond political rhetoric to include meaningful dialogue and understanding, the BJP under Modi's leadership seeks to bridge divides

within the Muslim community and foster a sense of belonging on a national scale. These initiatives underscore a commitment to inclusive governance and the empowerment of all sections of society, reinforcing Modi's vision for a more unified and harmonious India.

Modi's government has also launched the Shaadi Shagun scheme for the welfare of Muslim women. The scheme aims to encourage Muslim women to pursue higher education. An amount of Rs 51,000 will be granted to the muslim graduates who have received the Maulana Azad Education foundation scholarship. The Maulana Azad National Fellowship Scheme provides financial assistance to students from minority communities, to pursue higher education such as M.Phil and Ph.D.

Muslim-owned businesses registered under the Prime Minister's Employment Generation Program (PMEGP) have increased by 70 per cent since 2014. The percentage of Muslim children enrolled in schools has seen an increase from 69.4 per cent in 2014 to 74.2 per cent in 2019, passing the national average of 72.7 per cent. In addition, the gender gap in male enrollment has narrowed as well.

In the last nine years of Modi's rule, the number of muslim government employees has gone up from 4.5 per cent to 10.5 per cent. By 2021, more than 13 Lakh minority students, including Muslims, have received scholarships under the national scholarship schemes.

About 22 per cent people from the Muslim community prospered because of the Skill India Programme, which makes it the largest beneficiary of the scheme.

More than 42 per cent of the accounts opened under the flagship PM Jan Dhan Yojana are owned by Muslims, which is a shining example of the trust that the community puts in the Modi government and its steady progress since 2014.

International relations with Muslim Countries

Modi's popularity within the Muslim community also extends internationally. India enjoys a very healthy relationship with the Arab Countries. As a show of friendship, Iran removed visa requirements for Indian travellers. India also shares a very cordial relationship with Saudi Arabia. Recently, Saudi Crown Prince Mohammed bin Salman visited Delhi for the G20 Leaders' summit where he, along with Prime Minister Narendra Modi and USA President Joe Biden, announced the India-Middle East-Europe Economic Corridor.

During Prime Minister Modi's inaugural trip to Egypt, both nations inked four pacts, notably forging a 'strategic partnership.' Memorandums of Understanding (MoUs) covered agriculture, monument preservation, and competition laws, reflecting collaborative efforts spanning diverse sectors such as agriculture, heritage conservation, and legal frameworks. This signifies an important step towards fostering bilateral relations and mutual cooperation between India and Egypt.

Time and again, Modi has reiterated in his speeches that minorities have nothing to fear in India. He has repeated that the Muslim population has as many rights and freedom as the majority of Hindus in the country. The motto of the Modi government is Sabka Saath-Sabka Vikaas, and despite claims from elements that only want to talk about the negative aspect of governing a country, it seems to be succeeding so far.

PM Modi (L) being welcomed by the President of the UAE, Sheikh Mohamed bin Zayed Al Nahyan (R) at Qasr Al-Watan (Presidential Palace), in Abu Dhabi

PM Modi (L) conferred Order of the Distinguished Rule of Nishan Izzuddeen by Ibrahim Mohamed Solih (R), President of Maldives in Male

Prime Minister Narendra Modi (R) and Afgahnistan President Ashraf Ghani (L)

Prime Minister Modi and the Christian Community

PM Modi is just as concerned about the welfare of other minorities in the countries as well. He shares a warm relationship with the Indian christian community, celebrating Christmas with them every year.

He has praised Christian for their services to the poor and sick, and for guiding the country towards a path of goodness. Drawing similarities between the Bible and the Upanishads, he spoke about how the two religious texts serve as a guiding light for people. He also mentioned the importance of the Chritstian freedom fighters who helped free the country from the British.

Last year, the Leaders from the Christian community including Catholic, Protestant, and Eastern Orthodox leaders backed the government's dream of making India developed by 2047. Christians in India enjoy benefits of all the schemes that have been created for the welfare of the minorities.

Prime Minister Modi and the Sikh Community

Apart from Muslims and Christians, Modi also keeps the Sikh community in high esteem. Prime Minister Narendra Modi's administration took significant steps to address historical injustices and honour the Sikh community.

Under PM Modi's leadership, a Special Investigation Team (SIT) was formed to ensure justice for victims of the 1984 anti-Sikh riots. Over 300 cases were reopened, leading to the imprisonment of those found guilty. Additionally, the government provided financial support of Rs 5 lakh to 3,328 victim families, bringing some closure to their suffering. Efforts were made to restore the dignity of Sikh heritage, including the restoration of the Jallianwala Bagh memorial to its former glory. Through the Citizenship Amendment Act, Sikh brothers and sisters who faced persecution in Afghanistan and Pakistan were granted Indian citizenship, demonstrating a commitment to protecting religious minorities. In a symbolic gesture, December 26 was declared Veer Baal Diwas by the Modi government, honouring the bravery and principles exemplified by the four Veer Sahibzades of Guru Gobind Singh Ji. This day stands as a testament to India's commitment to preserving its cultural heritage and upholding the spirit of *Bhartiyata*.

All of these efforts put by the Modi government to alleviate and safeguard the minorities living in the country should be enough to dispel all wrong and misguided information about ill relations between them. PM Modi's vision of a united India remains strong as ever and won't be shaken by anti-national forces that want to divide and weaken our great democratic nation.

INDIA, THE VISHWAGURU

In his speeches over the years, PM Modi has highlighted India's role as the '*Vishwaguru*' in world affairs. *Vishwaguru* is a Sanskrit word which means world or global teacher. The word has become synonymous to Modi, and to India as well. A burgeoning economy, and the largest democracy in the world, India is a land of abundant knowledge which it is eager to share with people who are eager to learn.

In his own words, Modi has stated that India is now reaching new summits that had been impossible to achieve until now. At the occasion of the Chandrayaan launch, Modi declared that India is going to solve the biggest problems of the world.

To campaign for the G20 summit that was held in India in 2023, the government stamped posters that hailed Modi as the *Vishwaguru*, signalling to the foreign leaders his growing importance at the world stage.

At the BRICS Summit in South Africa, he mentioned how the country is taking leaps in terms of using technology to solve issues that plague the society.

'Public service delivery is being revolutionised through Digital Public Infrastructure Diversity is a great strength of India. The solution to any problem in India comes out at the test of this diversity. That's why these solutions can be easily implemented in any corner of the world. In this context, we will be happy to share all these platforms developed in India with BRICS partners.' He noted.

India has exported and spread its rich culture across the globe. Today, millions of people practise yoga daily to remain fit, an exercise that originated in this country and has been promoted by PM Modi as the secret to a long and healthy life.

Modi also promotes a value based politics and rule based order of governance. At a Shangri-La Dialogue, Modi spoke about the necessity of having a democratic and rule based order. He stated that rules and norms were needed to combat the uncertainty of the current times and to avoid running into rivalries with others. The order must be free and open, along with being equitable and inclusive. According to Modi, these factors will ensure that our governance is run smoothly, without any hindrance.